NAUM GABO

front cover
'Linear Construction in Space No.2'
1972/3 *Family Collection*

ISBN 0 946590 71 0
Published by order of the Trustees 1987
for the exhibition of 11 February – 20 April 1987
Copyright © 1987 The Tate Gallery All rights reserved
Designed and published by Tate Gallery Publications,
Millbank, London SW1P 4RG
Printed by The Hillingdon Press, Uxbridge, Middlesex

NAUM GABO

Sixty Years of Constructivism

THE TATE GALLERY

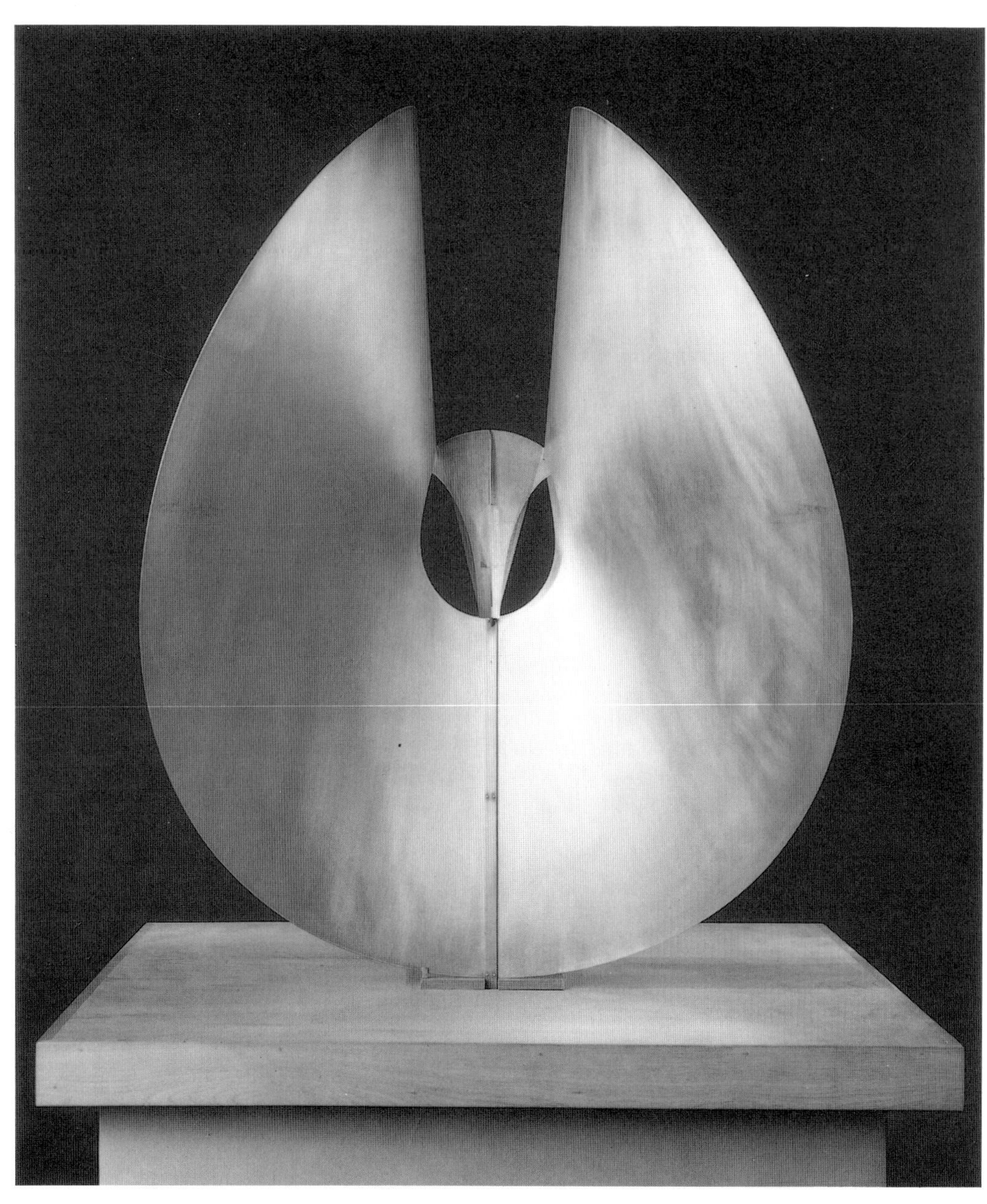

Bronze Spheric Theme 1960/1965
90cm high [cat.no.39]

Introduction

This exhibition is the third in a series that has been devoted to three masters of modern art who took refuge in this country during the last war. After Schwitters and Kokoschka, we now celebrate Gabo, the first to arrive in England, and the one who made the closest and most enduring link with English art. Gabo came in 1936 to work with the painter Ben Nicholson and the architect Leslie Martin on *Circle: International Survey of Constructive Art*, the one indisputable publication of major European importance to be produced in this country during the inter-war period. In 1939 he moved to St Ives in Cornwall, at the suggestion of Nicholson and his wife Barbara Hepworth, and it was his presence and his influence on such local artists as Peter Lanyon and John Wells that helped ensure that St Ives art would always be international and not parochial in its general outlook.

Gabo left England in 1946 to settle in the United States, but in a strange way he seemed to continue to exert a stronger personal influence in this country than in America. The strength of British constructivism in the 1950s and 1960s, and in particular the work of Pasmore, Kenneth and Mary Martin, Anthony Hill and others owes not a little to his example.

Towards the end of his life, Gabo was spending more and more of his time in London, and those who visited him in Camden Town will remember an unforgettable experience. Here was an artist whose career stretched back to the beginnings of modern art still active and full of the most original ideas and perception.

Gabo himself was exceptionally generous to this country, and his gifts to the Tate Gallery have left us with the most important collection of his work held by any museum. My predecessor, Sir Norman Reid, had a particular feeling for Gabo's work, and as a result the Tate Gallery has a remarkably complete collection of the small maquettes which were the kernel of Gabo's artistic thinking. These should be a permanent display: they are an important element in the Modern Sculpture Museum which will, we hope, be the next stage in the Tate Gallery's development plans.

The present exhibition was originally brought together by Steven Nash of the Dallas Museum of Art, and shown in Dallas, at the Art Gallery of Ontario, Toronto, and the Solomon R. Guggenheim Museum, New York. It was then, with the collaboration of Jörn Merkert of the Kunstsammlung Nordrhein-Westfalen, shown in Düsseldorf after first being seen at the Akademie der Künste, Berlin. We are very happy to use Steven Nash's comprehensive monograph on Gabo as a catalogue, but Michael Compton has added this most illuminating short guide to the Tate exhibition. He has also added a number of works, mainly from the Tate collection, and a complete supporting exhibition, the Graphic Archive. This latter is almost entirely from the collection of the family of the artist, who have lent extra works to the main exhibition, in addition to the very large number which have formed its core and substance throughout the tour. So, while extending the Gallery's thanks to all the generous lenders, I am glad again to acknowledge our immense debt to the artist's widow, Miriam Gabo, and to her daughter and son-in-law, Nina and Graham Williams, who have made all this possible.

Alan Bowness *Director*

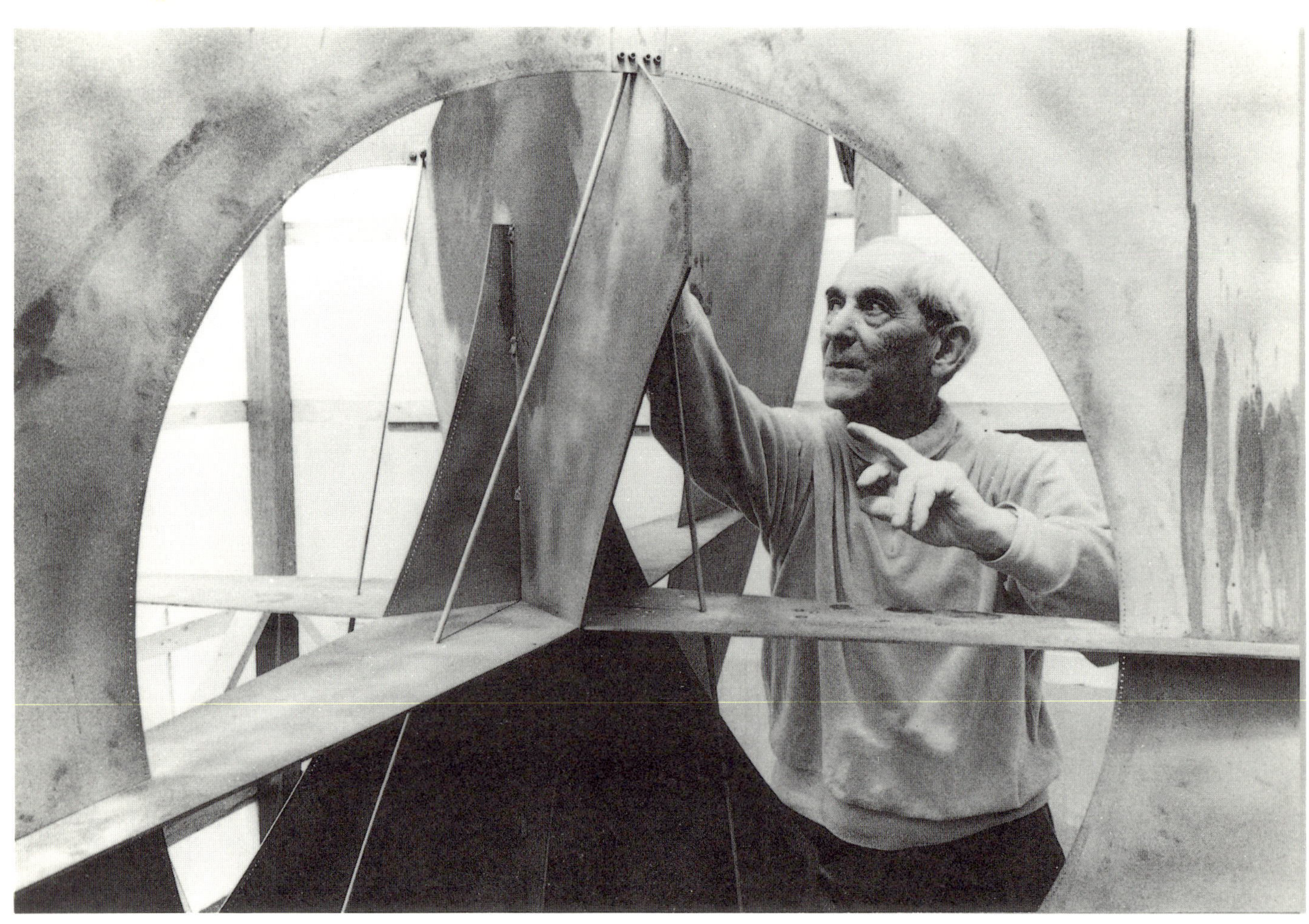

Naum Gabo working *c.* 1970 on **Spheric Theme** [cat.no.76]
Family Archive   photograph: Henri Cartier Bresson

Biography

Gabo was born on 4 August 1890 as Naum (or Neemia) Borisovich Pevsner in Bryansk, Russia, the son of the owner of a metals factory. His brothers included engineers and the painter Natan (later Antoine) Pevsner.

He was a lively, unruly and articulate boy who both wrote and painted from his teens. In 1910–13 he studied in Munich, dipping into Medicine, Engineering, Philosophy and Art history and travelling to Italy and France. He remained interested in the whole range of human thought and achievement. He was warm, open, contentious, humorous and highly individual.

As an enemy alien in Germany in 1914, as the war was about to begin, he moved to neutral Norway where he was joined by older and younger brothers Antoine and Alexei. Here in the city of Christiania (Oslo), far from the metropolis of the art world, he became an artist and renamed himself Gabo to distinguish himself from his brother.

In April 1917 all three brothers returned to Russia, supporting the Revolution that they hoped would lead to new freedoms. Gabo participated actively but informally in the outburst of argument and experiment in the arts that followed. He wrote and, with Antoine, published a 'Realist Manifesto' in 1920, one of the key documents in twentieth-century art. The two brothers staged an exhibition of their work.

In 1922 he went to Berlin as one of the organisers of the large official exhibition of Russian Art at the van Diemen Gallery, and stayed for ten years. During this period he established an international reputation and was invited, with Antoine, to design the ballet *La Chatte* for Diaghilev.

In 1932, anticipating the Nazi rise to power, he joined his brother in Paris. Gabo took an active part in the Paris-based *Abstraction-Création* group but was not happy there. He found the Paris art world rather complacent.

The preparation of an international exhibition, 'Abstract and Concrete', took him to London where he settled in 1936. He met and in 1937 married the American painter Miriam Israels. He quickly became a leading figure in British art helping to edit and contributing definitive articles to the manifesto volume *Circle*, also in 1937. He was introduced to the acrylic plastic material 'perspex' by Dr John Sisson of I.C.I.

In 1939 he joined Ben Nicholson and Barbara Hepworth in St Ives, Cornwall, which they established as a long lasting and creative artists' centre. His daughter Nina was born in 1941, and soon after the war, in 1947, Naum, Miriam and Nina settled in Woodbury, Connecticut. The family moved to Middlebury in 1953. He became an American citizen in 1952.

In his thirty years in the United States he ranked with the very great artists who had come from Europe, among them some whose notion of art was quite different, like his friend Marcel Duchamp. He had a number of important commissions including those from the Baltimore Museum of Art 1950, the Bijenkorf department store in Rotterdam, the Rockefeller Center, New York and St Thomas's Hospital, London. He taught, lectured and had several important retrospective exhibitions, one of which was shown at the Tate Gallery in 1966. After a second, smaller, exhibition in 1976 he gave an important group of works to the Tate including a large number of studies and models.

He received many honours but they did not deflect him from his work, which remained based in imagination, thought and practice and continued to develop new riches and subtleties until his death on 23 August 1977.

He retained a large proportion of his own work, including examples of most of the families of sculptures, which passed on to his wife and daughter. These are the basis of this exhibition, which is a tribute to his inventiveness, originality and sureness of eye.

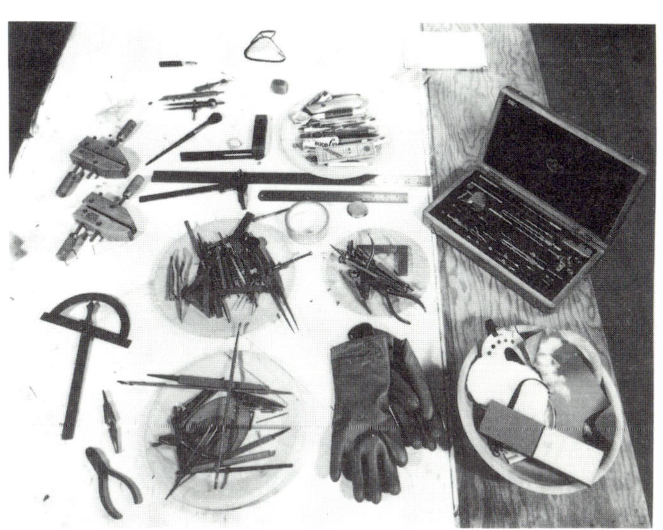

Gabo's worktable at Woodbury   *Family* /
photograph: Rudolph Burckhardt

The Realistic Manifesto, 1920

Above the tempests of our weekdays,

Across the ashes and cindered homes of the past,

Before the gates of the vacant future,

We proclaim today to you artists, painters, sculptors, musicians, actors, poets . . . to you people to whom Art is no mere ground for conversation but the source of real exaltation, our word and deed.

The impasse into which Art has come to in the last twenty years must be broken.

The growth of human knowledge with its powerful penetration into the mysterious laws of the world which started at the dawn of this century.

The blossoming of a new culture and a new civilisation with their unprecedented-in-history surge of the masses towards the possession of the riches of Nature, a surge which binds the people into one union, and last, not least, the war and the revolution (those purifying torrents of the coming epoch), have made us face the fact of new forms of life, already born and active.

What does Art carry into this unfolding epoch of human history?

Does it possess the means necessary for the construction of the new Great Style?

Or does it suppose that the new epoch may not have a new style?

Or does it suppose that the new life can accept a new creation which is constructed on the foundations of the old?

In spite of the demand of the renascent spirit of our time, Art is still nourished by impression, external appearance, and wanders helplessly back and forth from Naturalism to Symbolism, from Romanticism to Mysticism.

The attempts of the Cubists and the Futurists to lift the visual arts from the bogs of the past have led only to new delusions.

Cubism, having started with simplification of the representative technique ended with its analysis and stuck there.

The distracted world of the Cubists, broken in shreds by their logical anarchy, cannot satisy us who have already accomplished the Revolution or who are already constructing and building up anew.

One could heed with interest the experiments of the Cubists, but one cannot follow them, being convinced that their experiments are being made on the surface of Art and do not touch on the bases of it seeing plainly that the end result amounts to the same old graphic, to the same old volume and to the same decorative surface as of old.

One could have hailed Futurism in its time for the refreshing sweep of its announced Revolution in Art, for its devastating criticism of the past, as in no other way could one have assailed those artistic barricades of 'good taste' . . . powder was needed for that and a lot of it . . . but one cannot construct a system of art on one revolutionary phrase alone.

One had to examine Futurism beneath its appearance to realise that one faced a very ordinary chatterer, a very agile and prevaricating guy, clad in the tatters of worn-out words like 'patriotism', 'militarism', 'contempt for the female', and all the rest of such provincial tags.

In the domain of purely pictorial problems, Futurism has not gone further than the renovated effort to fix on the canvas a purely optical reflex which has already shown its bankruptcy with the Impressionists. It is obvious now to every one of us that by the simple graphic registration of a row of momentarily arrested movements, one cannot recreate movement itself. It makes one think of the pulse of a dead body.

The pompous slogan of 'Speed' was played from the hands of the Futurists as a great trump. We concede the sonority of that slogan and we quite see how it can sweep the strongest of the provincials off their feet. But ask any Futurist how does he imagine 'speed' and there will emerge a whole arsenal of frenzied automobiles, rattling railway depots, snarled wires, the clank and the noise and the clang of carouselling streets . . . does one really need to convince them that all that is not necessary for speed and for its rhythms?

Look at a ray of sun . . . the stillest of the still forces, it speeds more than 300 kilometres in a second . . . behold our starry firmament . . . who hears it . . . and yet what are our depots to those depots of the Universe? What are our earthly trains to those hurrying trains of the galaxies?

Indeed, the whole Futurist noise about speed is too obvious an anecdote, and from the moment that Futurism proclaimed that 'Space and Time are yesterday's dead', it sunk into the obscurity of abstractions.

Neither Futurism nor Cubism has brought us what our time has expected of them.

Besides those two artistic schools our recent past has had nothing of importance or deserving attention.

But Life does not wait and the growth of generations does not stop and we who go to relieve those who have passed into history, having in our hands the results of their experiments, with their mistakes and their achievements, after years of experience equal to centuries . . . we say . . .

No new artistic system will withstand the pressure of a growing new culture until the very foundation of Art will be erected on the real laws of Life.

Until all artists will say with us . . .

All is a fiction . . . only life and its laws are authentic and in life only the active is beautiful and wise and strong and right, for life does not know beauty as an aesthetic measure . . . efficacious existence is the highest beauty.

Life knows neither good nor bad nor justice as a measure of morals . . . need is the highest and most just of all morals.

Life does not know rationally abstracted truths as a measure of cognizance, deed is the highest and surest of truths.

Those are the laws of life. Can art withstand these laws if it is built on abstraction, on mirage, and fiction?

We say . . .

Space and time are re-born to us today.

Space and time are the only forms on which life is built and hence art must be constructed.

States, political and economic systems perish, ideas crumble, under the strain of ages . . . but life is strong and grows and time goes on in its real continuity.

Who will show us forms more efficacious than this . . . who is the great one who will give us foundations stronger than this?

Who is the genius who will tell us a legend more ravishing than this prosaic tale which is called life?

The realisation of our perceptions of the world in the forms of space and time is the only aim of our pictorial and plastic art.

In them we do not measure our works with the yardstick of beauty, we do not weigh them with pounds of tenderness and sentiments.

The plumb-line in our hand, eyes as precise as a ruler, in a spirit as taut as a compass . . . we construct our work as the universe constructs its own, as the engineer constructs his bridges, as the mathematician his formula of the orbits.

We know that everything has its own essential image; chair, table, lamp, telephone, book, house, man . . . they are all entire worlds with their own rhythms, their own orbits.

That is why we in creating things take away from them the labels of their owners . . . all accidental and local, leaving only the reality of the constant rhythm of the forces in them.

1. *Thence in painting we renounce colour as a pictorial element, colour is the idealised optical surface of objects; an exterior and superficial impression of them; colour is accidental and it has nothing in common with the innermost essence of a thing.*

We affirm *that the tone of a substance*, i.e. *its light-absorbing material body is its only pictorial reality.*

2. We renounce *in a line, its descriptive value: in real life there are no descriptive lines, description is an accidental trace of a man on things, it is not bound up with the essential life and constant structure of the body. Descriptiveness is an element of graphic illustration and decoration.*

We affirm *the line only as a direction of the static forces and their rhythm in objects.*

3. We renounce *volume as a pictorial and plastic form of space; one cannot measure space in volumes as one cannot measure liquid in yards; look at our space . . . what is it if not one continuous depth?*

We affirm *depth as the only pictorial and plastic form of space.*

4. We renounce *in sculpture, the mass as a sculptural element.*

It is known to every engineer that the static forces of a solid body and its material strength do not depend on the quantity of the mass . . . example a rail, a T-beam etc.

But you sculptors of all shades and directions, you still adhere to the age-old prejudice that you cannot free the volume of mass. Here (in this exhibition) we take four planes and we construct with them the same volume as of four tons of mass.

Thus we bring back to sculpture the line as a direction and in it we affirm a depth as the one form of space.

5. We renounce *the thousand-year-old delusion in art that held the static rhythms as the only elements of the plastic and pictorial arts.*

We affirm *in these arts a new element the kinetic rhythms as the basic forms of our perception of real time.*

These are the five fundamental principles of our work and our constructive technique.

Today we proclaim our words to you people. In the squares and on the streets we are placing our work convinced that art must not remain a sanctuary for the idle, a consolation for the weary, and a justification for the lazy. Art should attend us everywhere that life flows and acts . . . at the bench, at the table, at work, at rest, at play; on working days and holidays . . . at home and on the road . . . in order that the flame to live should not extinguish in mankind.

We do not look for justification, neither in the past nor in the future.

Nobody can tell us what the future is and what utensils does one eat it with.

Not to lie about the future is impossible and one can lie about it at will.

We assert that the shouts about the future are for us the same as the tears about the past: a renovated day-dream of the romantics.

A monkish delirium of the heavenly kingdom of the old attired in contemporary clothes.

He who is busy today with the morrow is busy doing nothing.

And he who tomorrow will bring us nothing of what he has done today is of no use for the future.

Today is the deed.

We will account for it tomorrow.

The past we are leaving behind as carrion.

The future we leave to the fortune-tellers.

We take the present day.

NAUM GABO
ANTOINE PEVSNER

Moscow, 5 August 1920   *2nd State Printing House*
Translation by Gabo © 1957

Rediscovered Sculptures

The most exciting happening in the last few years for those who love Gabo's work has been the re-emergence of a whole group that has not been seen for more than fifty years. Several of these are of a type, symmetrical with geometric, sometimes machine-like elements, of which the sculptures we have seen gave very little idea, although photographs were known. These pieces add much to our understanding of Gabo and of art in central Europe in the twenties, but are also of great individual beauty.

The surprise is that they were in Gabo's possession all the time, hidden in storerooms and boxes. One little bit that had been separated had become a sculpture on its own, until its proper place was found.

The phenomenon of their reappearance is partly due to Gabo's method of working and to the events of his life. His technique of constructing sculpture out of flat elements meant that they could be taken to pieces and packed away into a small volume. This could be a great convenience to a sculptor – the young Modigliani, for example, had had to tip his accumulated sculpture into the river when he left Livorno for Paris, unable to afford either to move it or have it stored. Gabo himself moved again and again: Oslo, Moscow, Berlin, Paris, London, Connecticut. Most of these works must have been packed up for his move to Paris under threat of the Nazis and have not been seen publicly since.

The reason why they did not get put together again is suggested by Gabo's own words which apply to several sculptures in the group:

> My works of this time, up to 1924, are all in the search for an image which would fuse the sculptural element with the architectural element into one unit. I consider this column [No.10] the culmination of that search.

During his lifetime Gabo showed few early sculptures in his retrospective exhibitions; 'Head No.2', 'Head No.3', 'Column' and 'Construction in Space with Balance on Two Points' were the ones exhibited most often. These, for him, summed up whole phases of his work. In the case of the architectural group the simplicity and directness of 'Column' and 'Construction in Space with Balance on Two Points' and the absence of machine references must have made them, at least in retrospect, the decisive works.

The machine associations, on the other hand, are typical of the spirit of the twenties in Russia, Germany and France. They date the works and at the same time evoke that period in which industry was seen in a Utopian light. Gabo was an artist for whom the purpose of art was to state a vision for his time and for the future. In several of these works we see him associating that vision with the aesthetic of the machine, an idea he was quickly to transcend.

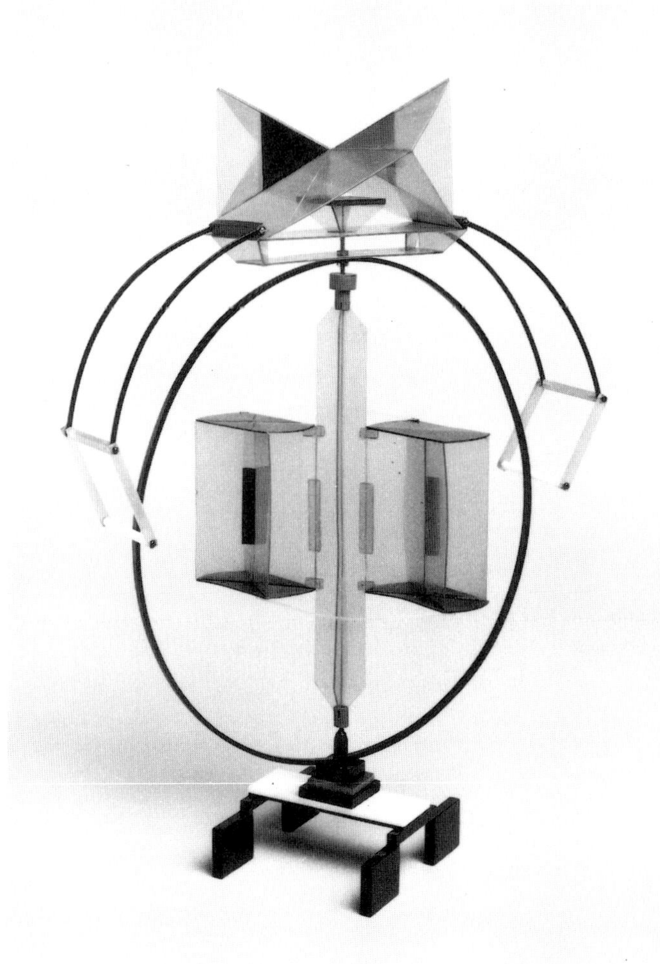

Model for 'Rotating Fountain' 1925/reassembled 1986
54cm high [cat.no.18] *Family Collection*

We should pay here a tribute to Gabo's family and friends, who recognised and discovered the pieces, including Professor Charles Wilson who also reassembled them. He was able to use photographs to locate the parts which had sometimes been dispersed, However it is amazing how very few of the little pieces of metal, glass or plastic had disappeared or have not been certainly identified and have had to be remade. But Charles Wilson had also worked for many years helping Gabo to construct his sculptures. His understanding of the artist made it possible for him to interpret all the clues, including symmetries and the marks of fixing, to resurrect these wonderful sculptures just as they were and to give us the excitement of seeing them with so much of Gabo's other work.

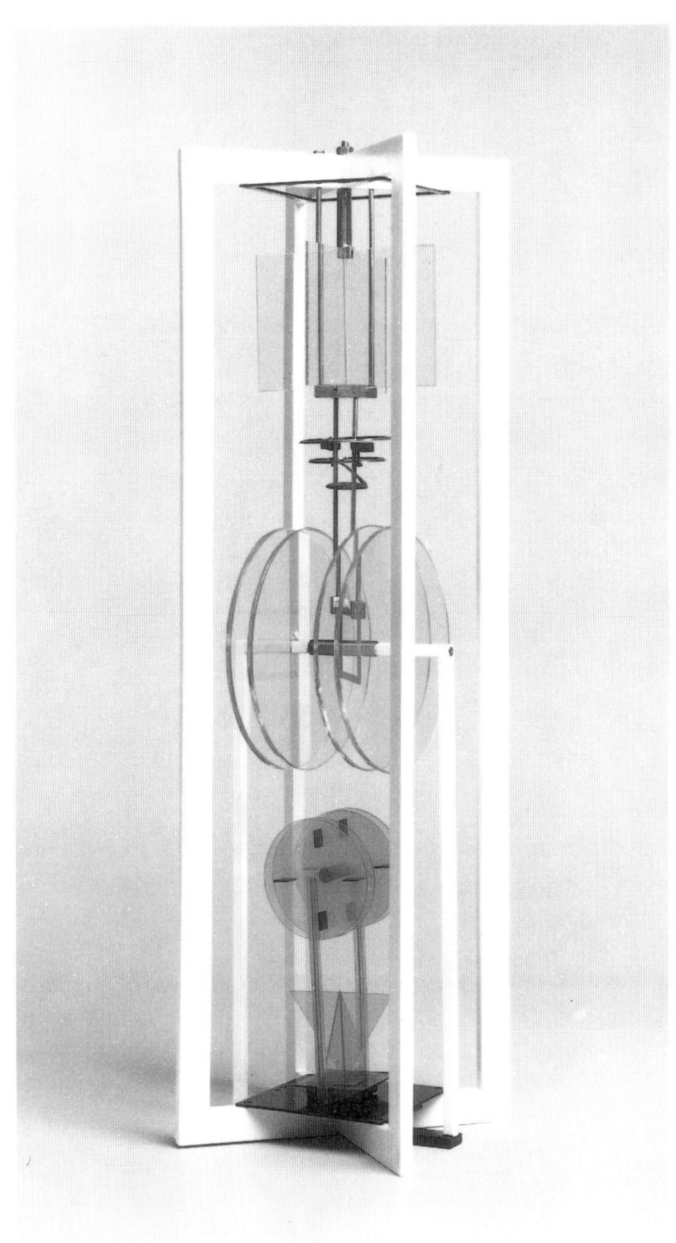

Construction in Space: Diagonal 1921–25 / reassembled 1986
62.2cm high [cat.no.14]   *Family Collection*

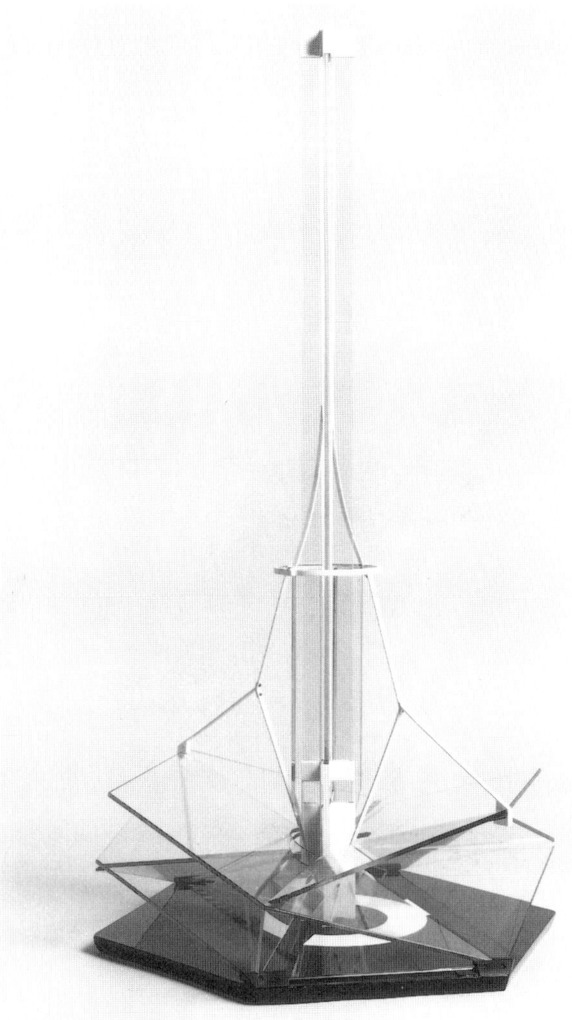

Construction in Space: Vertical 1923–5 / reassembled 1986
120cm high [cat.no.15]   *Family Collection*

Gallery Guide

The exhibition is laid out in an open plan so that the sculptures may have space round them and so that visitors may see almost the whole range of Gabo's work from any position. For Gabo was not an artist who developed his work in a straight line, discarding what went before, but one who constantly reworked and redeveloped his ideas. Nevertheless it is possible to walk round the galleries following more or less consistently the chronological development of his art and it is this development which is described here.

First Bay

This bay contains Gabo's earliest drawings and paintings and the sculpture conceived, and often constructed, in Norway where he sheltered during the war years, 1914-17. In this short period, away from the centres of the art world, he matured rapidly as an artist. He made many drawings but realised few works, preferring to develop them carefully. In this way he achieved, almost at the first attempt, sculptures which have been capable of re-creation on a grand scale and in a variety of materials. They are some of the most assured and the most striking images in twentieth century art.

His sculptures were made first on a small scale in card cut out and glued together. This model was then constructed on a larger scale in industrial materials such as plywood or steel and later plastic. The sculptures spring principally from cubist painting of about 1910–11 and may be considered as an attempt to 'correct' Cubism, to work it out in three dimensions and to turn it to new, personal ends.

Among them 'Constructed Head No.2' (cat.nos.2–4) is perhaps the definitive work. It is shown here in three versions, the latest executed in 1966, half a century after the first, and four times as large. In this sculpture, first constructed in 1916, Gabo succeeded in representing a human form not as surface and mass, but in terms of the space that it occupies. However he was not a scientist but an artist and he shows great skill in making the head interesting and expressive from all viewpoints without borrowing detail and expression from any individual head.

'Constructed Head No.3' (cat.no.5) is in the form of a relief, conceived in Norway but first constructed in Moscow where Gabo went soon after the revolution of February 1917. Drawings and photographs show that he worked on a number of reliefs, which evolved rapidly to a type of abstract Cubism (cat.nos.100, 101) in which the traces of the head or other natural forms are eliminated, but the irregular rhythms of representation remain.

Gabo found himself for a short while in tune with the extraordinary surge of experimentation that animated the studios and schools of Moscow in the ferment following the February and October Revolutions. Artists sought to create a new art by exploring the fundamentals of their

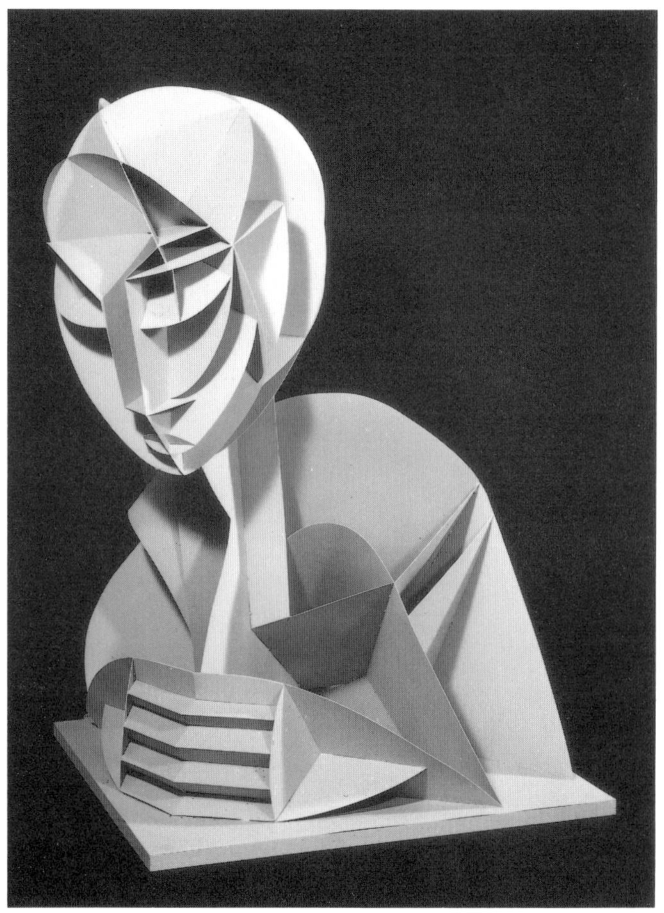

Constructed Head No.2 1916/1923–4
43cm high [cat.no.3]   *Family Collection*

craft and medium; at the same time they aimed to play a more direct role in building a new society.

Among the materials which Gabo took up was one that was to be his prime medium for the rest of his life, clear plastic. He was no doubt excited by its modernity and by the way it modulates light – reflecting, refracting and transmitting. But it was also the solution to his formal problem, for it allowed the whole of a three-dimensional work to be seen from a single viewpoint and yet it provided infinite variety as the viewpoint moved. He seems to have used it first in a relief of 1920 (now lost) in which, by these means, he passed through Cubism; for in paint, multiple viewpoints had to be presented simultaneously, and the result had been impossible to read directly.

By solving his 'problem' in representation, Gabo was liberated from it and could practise construction as freely and imaginatively as he was able, very soon making use of opaque as well as clear plastics and shiny metals.

Second Bay

Gabo saw at once the analogy between his constructed sculpture and architecture; like other Russian artists, he began to draw and model towers and monuments. Some of these have the floating structure of cubist painting (cat. no.98), but others become much more feasible as structures. They seem to have parts which rotate around one another, sweeping out planes and volumes in space (cat. nos.103–108). He made a single sculpture to demonstrate this idea, his 'Kinetic Construction (Standing Wave)' (cat. no.8). In its perfect simplicity it defines a new concept of space in art and with it Gabo created one of the icons of twentieth-century sculpture.

By 1920 Gabo had found that he had an infinite resource in shape, structure, rhythm, implied or actual motion and in the qualities of his materials. He dispensed forever with representation in favour of construction, and wrote his Realistic Manifesto, signed also by his brother Antoine and published in August 1920.

Almost contemporary with this, and complementary to it, is the model for 'Column'. The structure is clear-cut and symmetrical; instead of the curved surface of a cylinder (implied by the disc base and the tilted ring) you see two tall, intersecting, rectangular planes that define the same volume. The method, called by Gabo 'stereometric', is a simplified version of the one he had used in 'Constructed Head No.2' (cat.nos.2–4). The same purer geometry is seen in his reliefs of about 1920 such as cat.no.12.

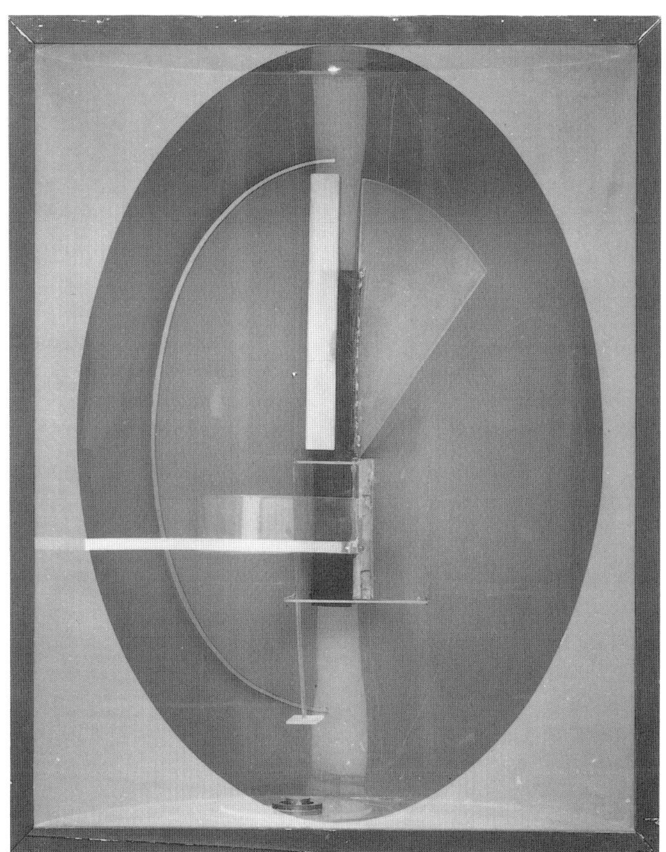

Red Cavern *c.*1926
66cm high [cat.no.21]

Third Bay

These themes continued to preoccupy Gabo when he moved to Berlin in 1922. He made a series of works in the form of hypothetical towers, monuments or fountains. The parts of these are mostly in the form of elementary Euclidean figures: circles, rectangles, triangles – shapes that may suggest machinery. But they are classical in the clarity of their composition: the dominance of horizontal and vertical, their symmetry about a vertical axis. With these works Gabo participated in the 'return to order' which affected all Europe in the early 1920s, following the eruption of Cubism and Expressionism, the turmoil of war and revolution. He imagined tower blocks topped with airports for vertical take-off aeroplanes, a new town and, for a competition, a Palace of the Soviets. He invented and patented a roof-structure capable of spanning vast areas. Some of this work is exhibited in the archive display at the entrance to the exhibition.

On a more modest scale, he projected sculptural reliefs for an architectural setting. These may take the form of a dynamically curved construction in a shallow box or niche which isolates their space from that of the room in which they hang ('Red Cavern' (cat.no.21) and 'Construction in a Niche' (cat.no.27)). In this way they develop the concept of the corner relief of 1916–17.

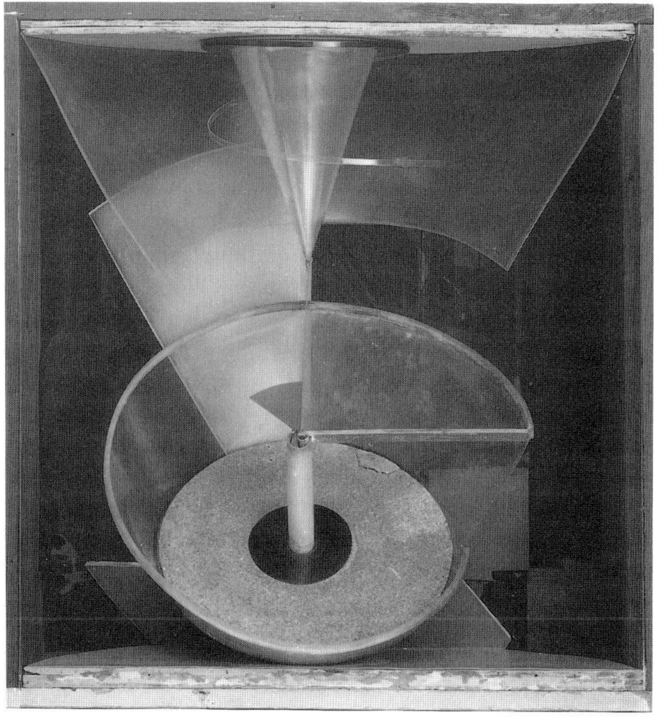

Construction in a Niche 1930
61 × 28 × 58.5cm [cat.no.27]

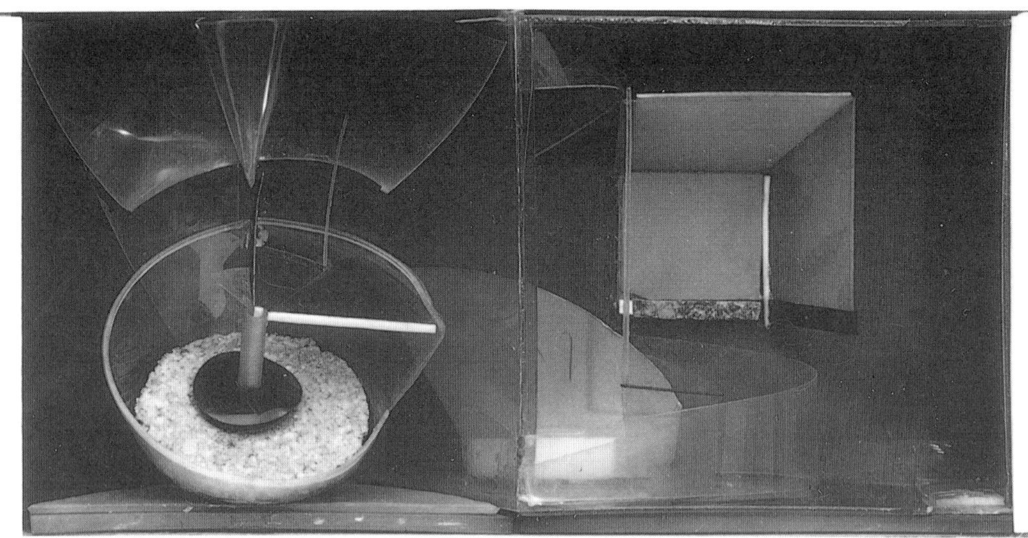

Model for 'Double Relief in a Niche' 1929–30
[detail cat.no.26]

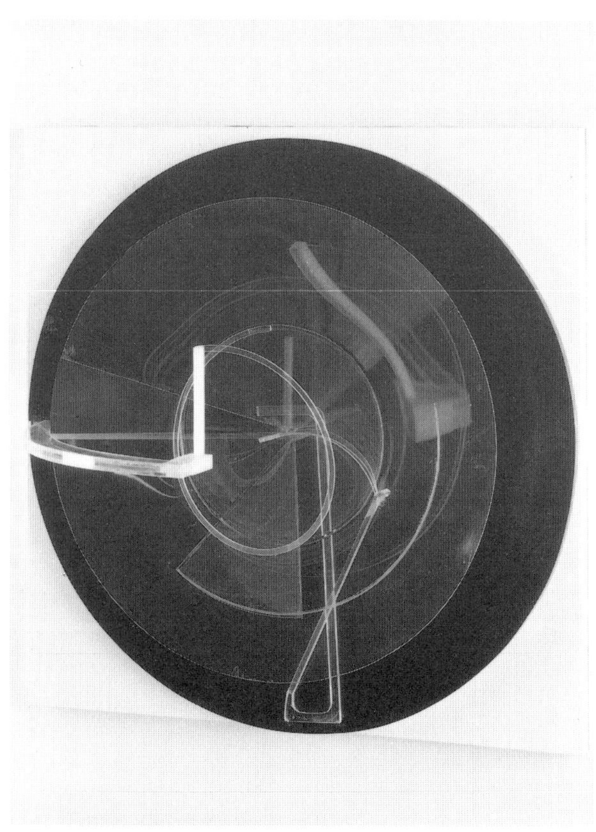

Circular Relief *c.*1925
50 × 50 × 23cm [cat.no.20]

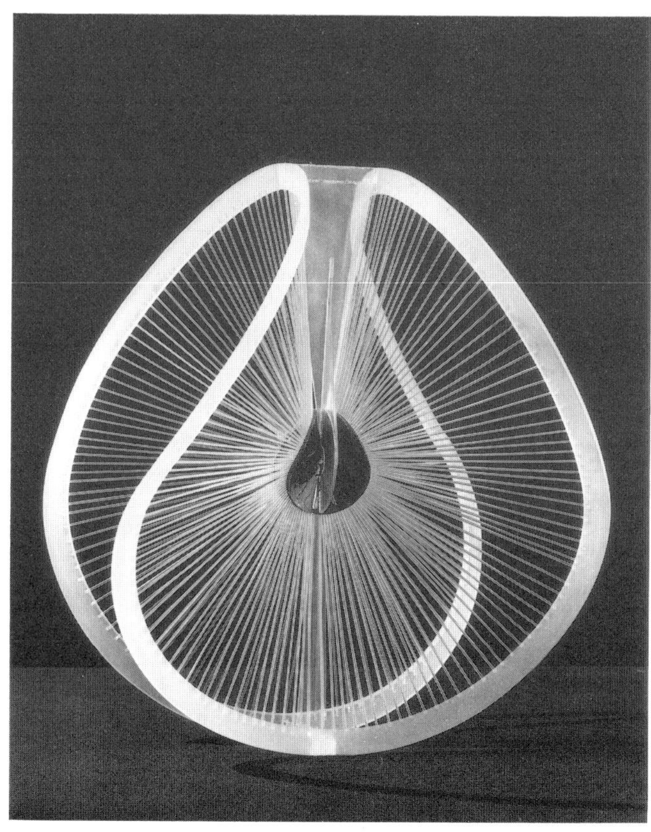

Spheric Theme 2nd Variation 1937–8
43.5cm high [cat.no.36] *Family Collection*

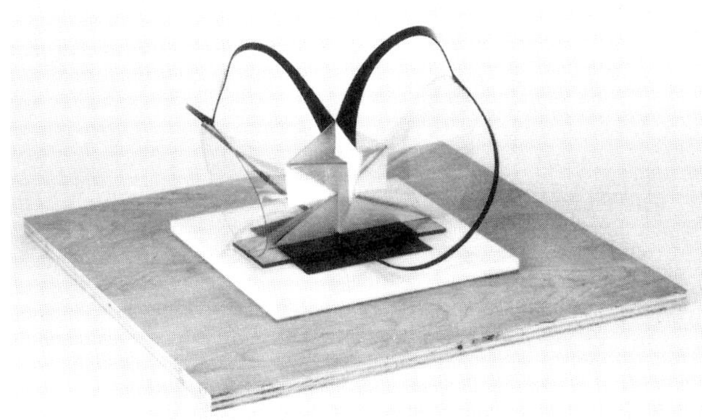

Construction in Space: 'Two Cones' 1927/1968
26.7cm high [cat.no.24]

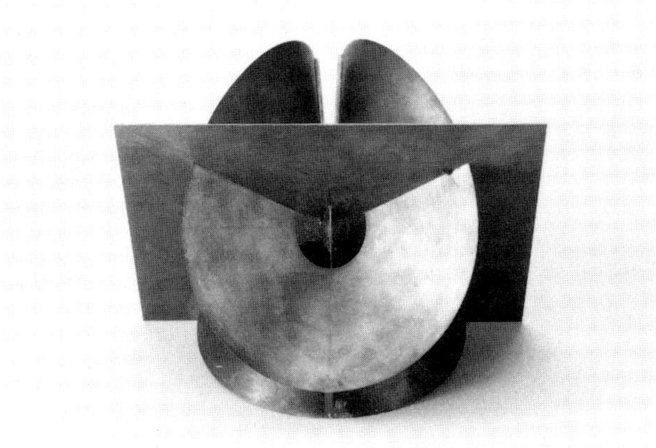

Spheric Theme (Penetrated Variation) 1963–5
33cm high [cat.no.38]

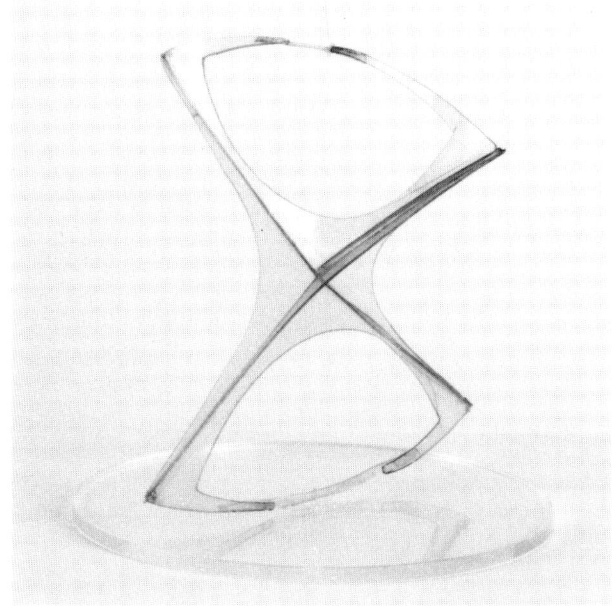

Model for 'Torsion' *c.*1928–9
8.9 × 9.5cm diameter [cat.no.25]

Fourth Bay

Gabo's largest structure was the set for Diaghilev's ballet *La Chatte* of 1927, which he devised with the help of his brother Antoine Pevsner. Its sweeping, glittering transparent forms are closely related to Gabo's reliefs and to his models for fountains and monuments. The model for the set has recently been reassembled and restored (cat.nos. 22 and 114–119). The element of movement in this work was provided, of course, by the dancers, the music and the stage lighting. In this way it is parallel to the more static constructions in the Second Bay which would have been enlivened by jets and cascades of water, rays of light and radio, air traffic and natural phenomena.

But Gabo also sought to imply movement in the form and rhythm of the sculpture itself, which seems to resonate and echo in the space around it. This appears in a very simple form in 'Monument for an Airport' (cat.no.19), with its rhombuses. The movement here is implied by the angles and by the overlapping forms. But the principle comes into its own in the late 1920s and 1930s. Dynamic curves replace the more static arcs in 'Construction in Space: Arch' (cat.no.29) and 'Model for Construction in Space: Two Cones' (cat.no.23), where planes are twisted and interlock. Gabo demonstrated in 'Construction: Stone with a Collar' (cat.no.31) and 'Kinetic Stone Carving (cat. no.32) that he could embody the idea in the most traditional medium. However, the key work in this phase is 'Spheric Theme', which first appears as a sculpture in miniature about 1937 (cat.nos.33 and 113, which shows the birth of the idea). The basic form was made by taking two identical flat pierced circles or broad rings and making a single cut in each along the line of a radius. The two discs are then bent in a serpentine curve and butt-jointed to each other at both ends. The resulting figure fits exactly into a sphere and the outer edges of the discs form the interlocking curves like those that divide the pieces of felt covering a tennis ball. This invention of Gabo's is a way of representing a sphere that is partly analogous to the stereometric device of his early sculptures, in that a volume is defined by planes at right angles to it.

At the same time it implies the range of ever increasing possible spheres – an expanding universe. But the internal space is also infinite, since the band comes back on itself while constructing the volume (unlike, for example, two discs set at right angles to each other). The whole sphere is made up of two interlocking volumes, defined by each of the two surfaces of the band. The volumes are identical but the axis of one is turned at ninety degrees to the other. The curvature of the planes constantly reverses from concave to convex and back to concave and so on forever. The form has the succinct structure and universal implication of a Yin Yang diagram imagined in three dimensions. 'Spheric Theme' was considered as a fountain like 'Torsion' (cat.no.73), which can likewise be fitted into a sphere. Over the years, Gabo constructed it in many different sizes, in a variety of materials and placed it in several attitudes.

Its structure could be made more rigid by inserting flat planes and these could be made to articulate its space. He could cut away parts of the discs and alter the twist. It could represent metaphorically the universe or an atom. It could seem like a theorem or a head. Other examples and ideas are shown in the archive display.

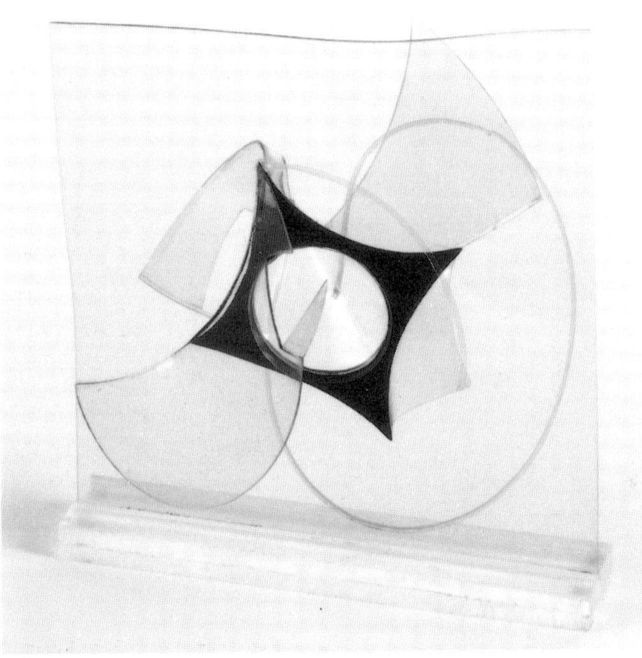

Construction on a Plane 1937
48 × 48 × 19.6cm [cat.no.40]

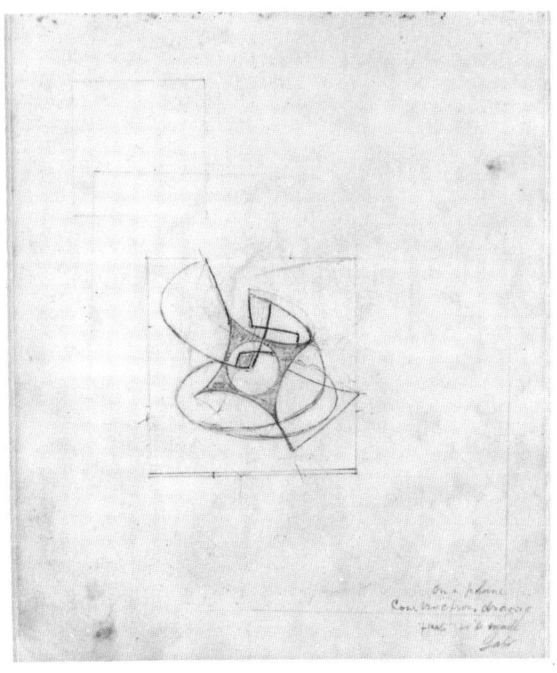

Sketch for 'Construction through a Plane'
1935 24.1 × 20.5cm [cat.no.129]

Fifth Bay

The title and character of 'Construction on a Plane' (cat. no.40) show that in 1937 Gabo was thinking more about universal concepts than of monuments or fountains. Such works take up again the theme of the lost 'Construction in Space C' but the curves are more subtle and suggest the infinite rather than the definite; space, even the space set up by the plane itself, is curved. Forms are represented almost as much by cutting out as by positive construction in 'Construction on a Line' (cat.no.41). The negative forms of this sculpture appear in positive/negative variations in 'Construction in Space with Crystalline Centre' (cat.no.44) and 'Spiral Theme' (cat.no.47). The extra brilliance of many of the works dating from about 1937 is due to the fact that Gabo was introduced to the use of the new plastic 'Perspex' – an acrylic sheet – at this time. This plastic can be easily twisted or bent but Gabo preferred to use it flat.

Some versions of 'Spheric Theme' are marked with radiating lines engraved on the surfaces. These lines emphasise and articulate the curvatures and seem to imply an angular velocity. Such lines are seen on some mathematical models made to illustrate complex equations so that they can be better understood by students. In 1937 Gabo was once more looking at such models. He even made a sculpture from one, 'Construction in Space: Crystal' (cat. no.43). Gabo was uniquely interested in this model because of its asymmetry and no doubt its unexpectedness, but it also interested the Surrealists who included it in an exhibition of Surrealist objects in Paris. It is a mathematical development of a cubic ellipse but Gabo extended the original to open up the curves in the way he had done with such reliefs as 'Construction on a Line' (cat.no.41).

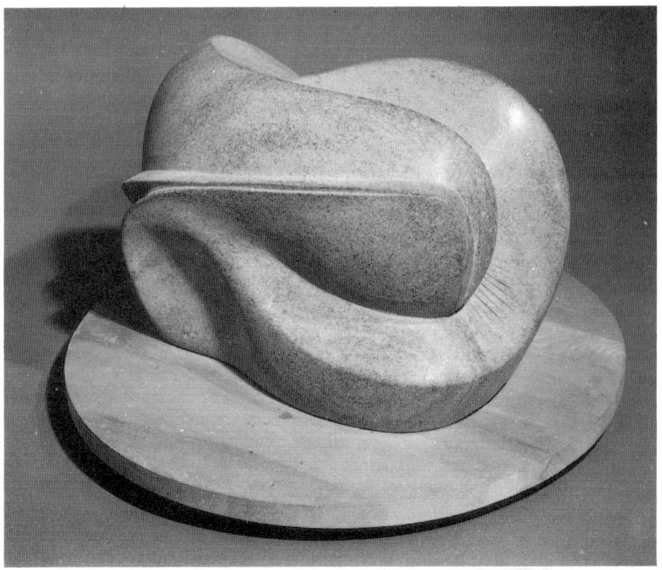

Kinetic Stone Carving 1936–44
24 × 37cm [cat.no.32]   *Family Collection*

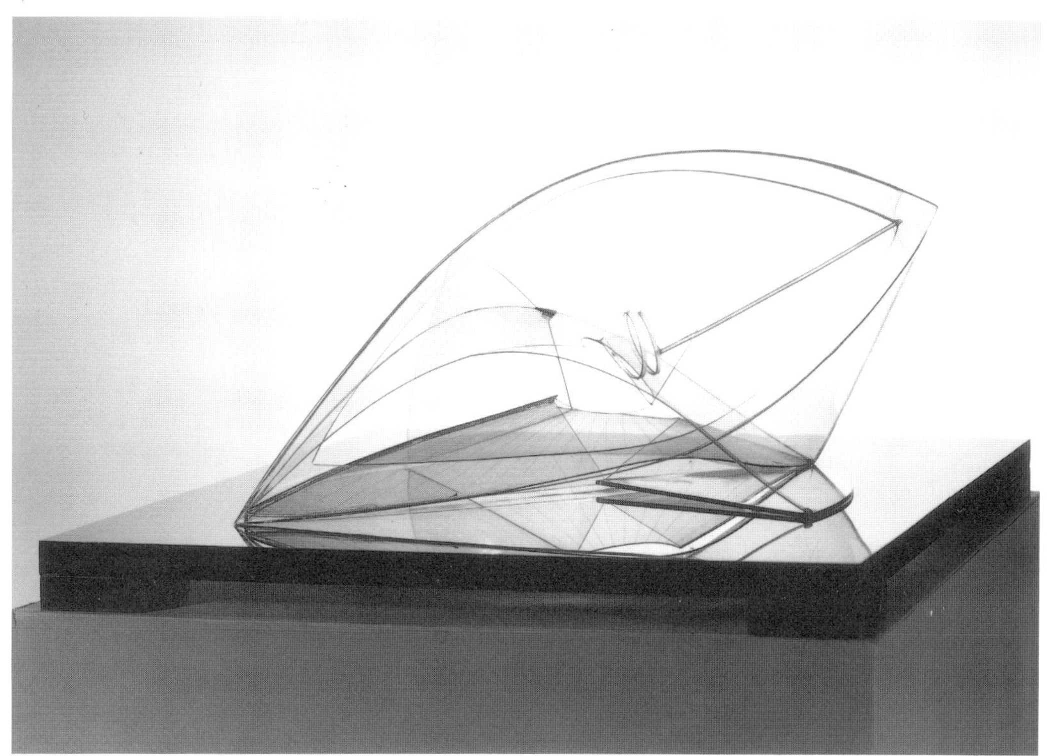

Spiral Theme 1941 14cm high [cat.no.47]

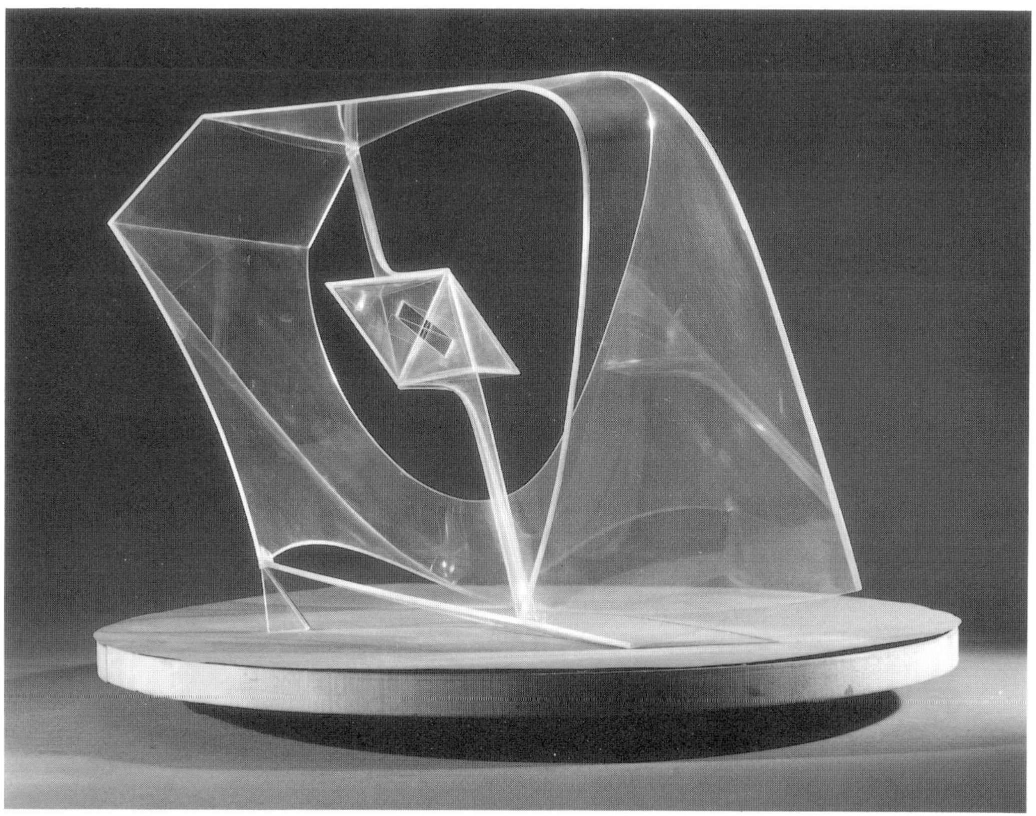

Construction in Space with Crystalline Centre
1938–40 32cm high [cat.no.44]   *Family Collection*

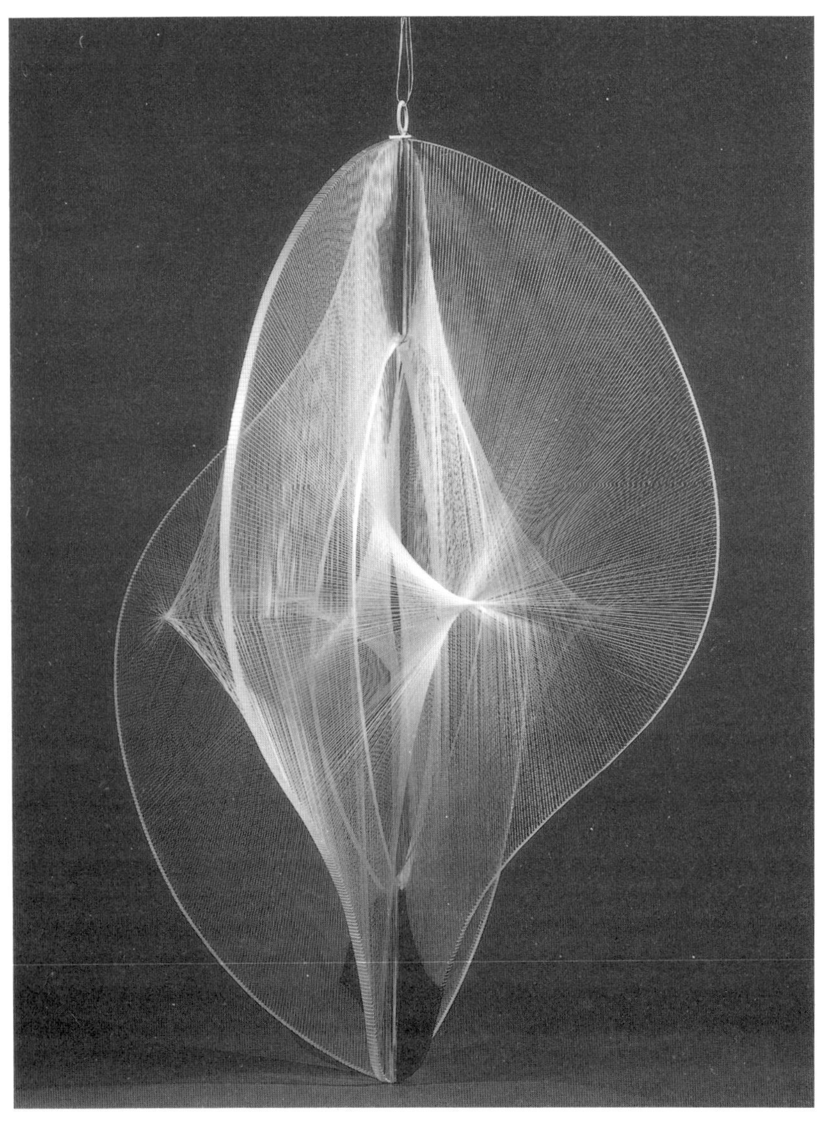

Linear Construction in Space No.2
1949/1972–3 92cm high [cat.no.52]

Sixth Bay

Some of the models made by mathematicians have surfaces defined by strings in a way that is related to these engraved lines. Gabo took up this idea and perfected it in the series 'Linear Constructions in Space' (cat.nos.48–51). They comprise a box-like framework of clear flat plastic sheet with a square inner diaphragm pierced by an oblique ellipse. The curved surfaces are formed by threading plastic filament between the adjacent elements of the framework. The theme of an ellipse in a square is related to that of 'Construction in Space: Crystal' (cat.no.43) but Gabo again achieves in terms of art (rather than of science) an image which is simplified, entirely self-contained (representing nothing) and yet having implications of universality and infinity. It is more crystalline than 'Crystal' itself. Gabo developed a related idea in solid form in the series represented here by cat.nos.45 and 46.

'Linear Construction in Space No.1' (cat.nos.48–51) is the definitive work of Gabo's period in England (where he arrived in 1936), but he continued to make versions of it in the United States, after he moved there in 1946. In America he produced at once another work of crystalline clarity, 'Linear Construction in Space No.2' (cat.nos.52, 53). This is formed round a structure of two flat planes set at right angles to one another – his basic 'stereometric' device. Each is a kind of ellipse of which alternate quarters become a hollow curve (his device of reversal). Within the plane is cut a negative ellipse, and the complex external surface is created by diagonal stringing.

His wife Miriam was a painter and, in the 1940s, Gabo again took up painting, a medium that he had used little since 1914. His pictures are of interlacing, dynamic curves, which with their carefully orchestrated colour evoke curved spaces. In painting he was able sometimes to articulate not only more complex structures than he had as yet executed in three dimensions, but also to imply echoes of the structures that animate the surrounding space.

Seventh Bay

In the United States Gabo's circumstances began to change slowly. He sold more pieces and could employ assistants to help him fabricate them. He received commissions for large works in public spaces. But he had always thought on a large scale and he continued in these works to develop the themes which he had already invented in small models, adding new ideas from time to time and considering carefully the architectural context. 'Construction in Space, with Net' (cat.no.55) and 'Model for a "Monument to the Unknown Political Prisoner"' (cat.no.56) are both developments from 'Spheric Theme'. The basic discs are carved or extended into more complex forms with inward and outward curving edges: cat.no.56 is greatly extended in the vertical dimension so that it becomes a dynamic metamorphosis of the early 'Column' (cat.no.10).

'The Bijenkorf Model' (cat.no.59) is a further development of this theme but the joints of the lamina are folded tight, giving a sharper silhouette. In 'Construction in Space: Arch No.2' (cat.no.65) the basic motif of 'Spheric Theme' appears once again but carved into still more complex shapes. The structure thus created is unmistakably biomorphic. It makes very clear the point that Gabo's constructions are analogues of those universal generative principles that shape not only atoms and nebulae but seeds and flowers, crystals, shells and works of art.

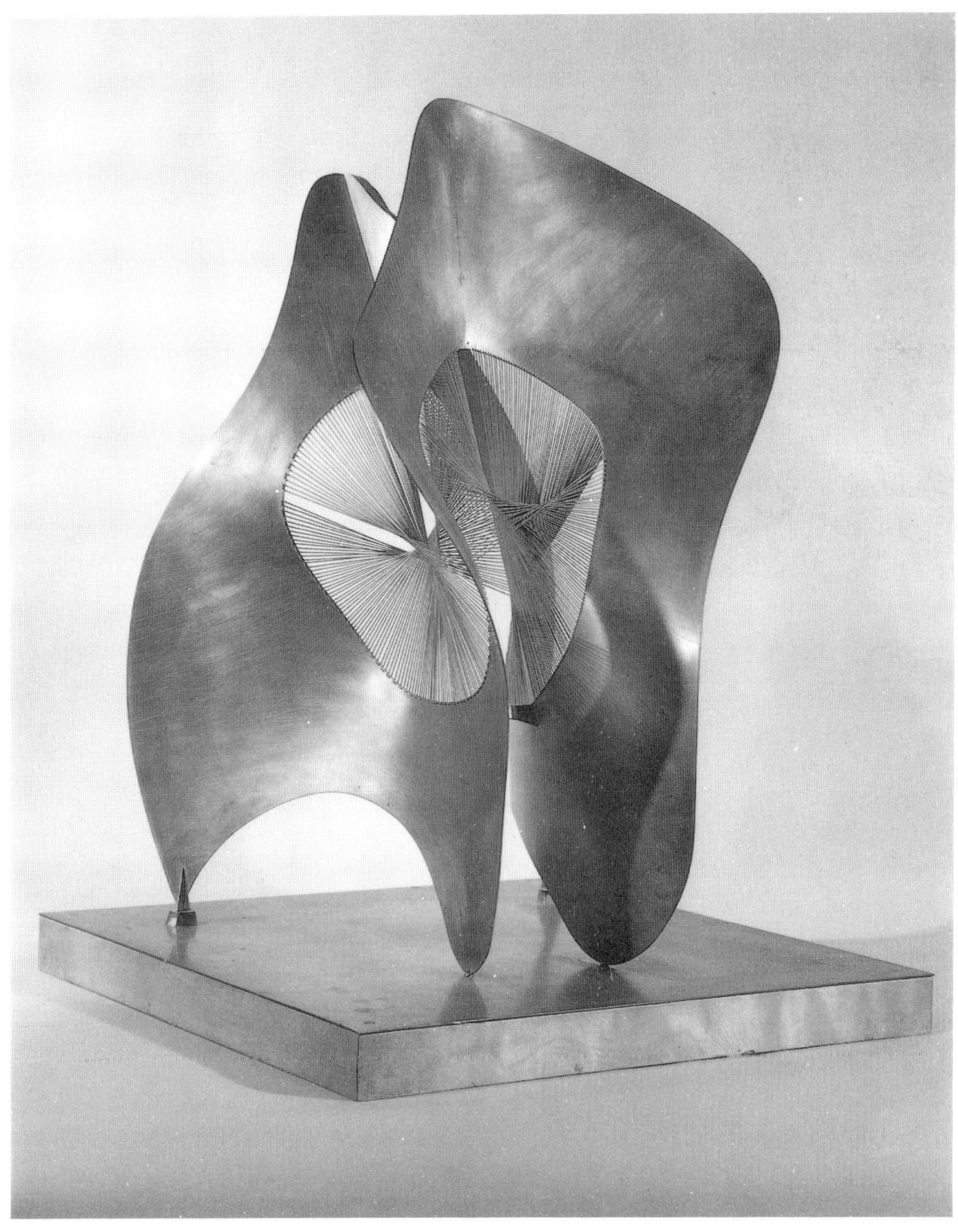

**Construction in Space:
Arch No.2** 1958/1963
82.6cm high [cat.no.65]
Family Collection

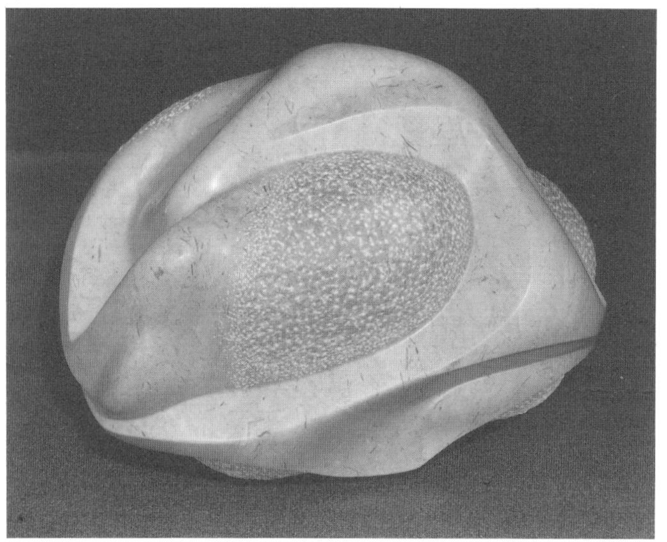

Quartz Stone 1964–65
80cm high [cat.no.70]   *Family Collection*

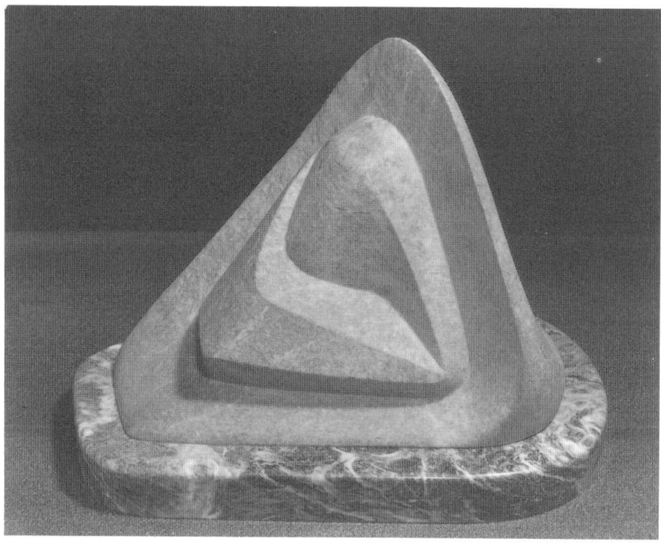

White Stone 1963–4
46cm high [cat.no.69]   *Family Collection*

Eighth Bay

A work of 1950 ('Baltimore Hanging Construction', not in the exhibition) is a cellular structure of curved and twisted planes reduced to an open framework. This theme, too, was developed by Gabo in the 1950s and 1960s to produce his most complex strung figures. These are again made of flat plastic or metal sheet cut into more elaborate curves and put together at right angles in the 'stereometric' manner. The stringing may be external, internal, or a combination of these. The result has the unity of biological or nuclear forms. The profiles of the structural elements were made, necessarily by cutting away external and internal shapes. Gabo could treat these as forms in their own right. The holes of the drill at the top of the two elements of 'Optical Relief' (cat.no.54) show that these were cut away to make the inner profile of such a work as 'Linear Construction in Space No.4' (cat.no.60). The biological analogy in his work is equally manifest in his powerful carving of the 1960s in which movement or growth is implied both by sweeping curves and by the stepped profiles which seem to be generated by the inner planes of the kind literally present in his constructed work. In 'Red Stone' (cat.no.72), for example, these set up a rapid rhythm, harmonically related to the whole.

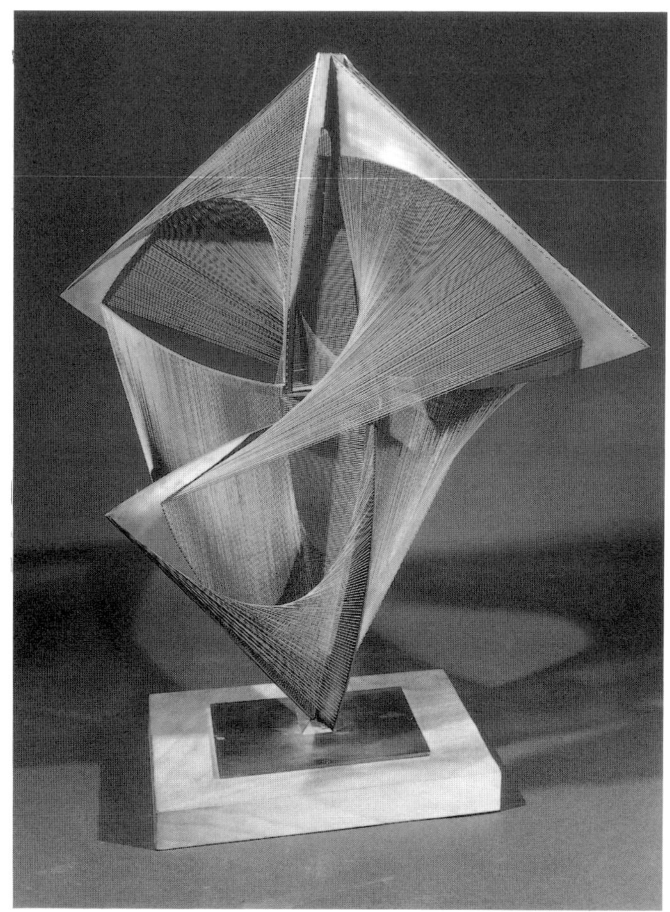

Torsion Variation 1962/1974–5
73.1cm high [cat.no.66]   *Family Collection*

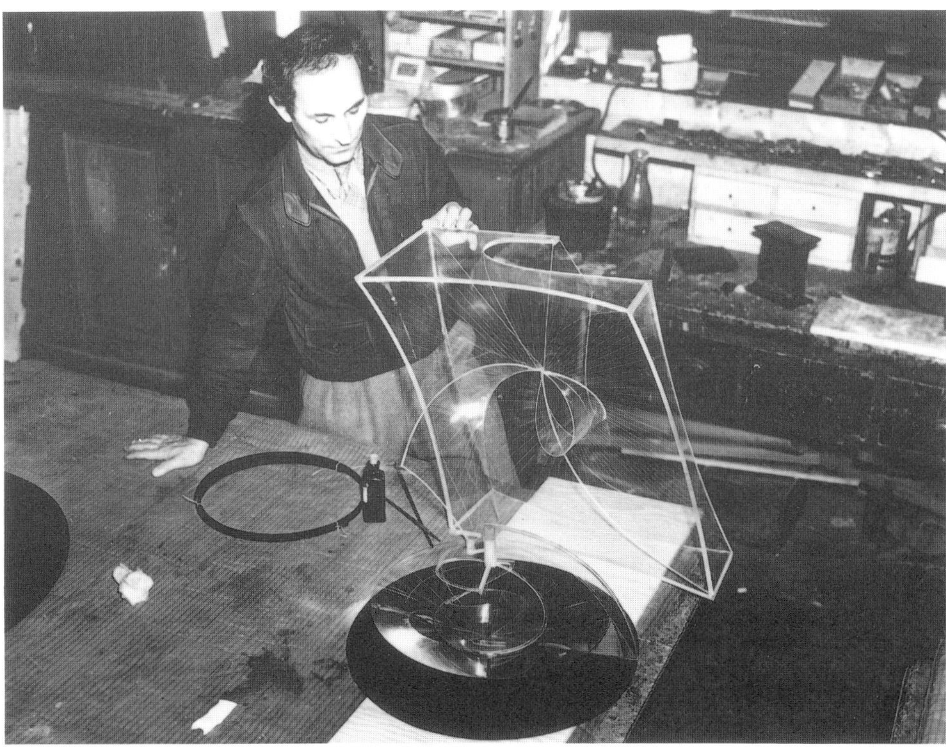

Gabo at the Wadsworth Atheneum 1938
with **Construction in Space: Crystal**
Family Archive

Ninth Bay

From about 1950 until the end of his life Gabo made mono-prints using engraved wood blocks, of which a small sample is shown here. The lines and forms are clearly related to those of the constructed works, although the prints are not representations of structures and are not literally construct-able. Gabo considered them to be a form of carving and used cut-out profiles, as well as drawing in pencil, in devis-ing them and cutting the blocks, but he was quickly in-volved in the medium and constantly experimented with the effects that could be achieved in the processes of ink-ing and printing, as well as with the blocks of wood them-selves and with the paper. Each print is unique. These wood engravings are a clear manifestation of the primacy of his aesthetic drive.

Finally this bay contains a grand and ultimate state-ments of his 'Spheric Theme' of which cat.no.76 is the final manifestation of the very first idea for 'Spheric Theme' (cat.no.33) of its most classic form. They stand here to represent the essence of his idea and purpose as a sculptor.

Graphic Archive

This display of drawings, models and objects made by Gabo has two linked sections. One is intended to show something of how Gabo conceived his work, the other represents his architectural and design projects.

Both groups are drawn principally from the 'Graphic Archive' assembled by Nina (Gabo) Williams and her husband Graham Williams from the material left by the artist. This does not generally include manuscripts, corres-pondence or personalia on the one hand or finished drawings on the other, but it is full of intriguing evidence of the artist at work. We have included, in addition, some pieces from among those given by Gabo to the Tate in his lifetime that have the same quality.

Drawings and Models

Except perhaps in his first phase as a sculptor, Gabo did not work out sculptural projects in drawing and then construct them; he rarely even used perspectival sketches as a starting point. But drawing was an integral part of his practice as an artist and he adpated or invented a number of graphic conventions as he needed them. Some of these are illustrated here or in the exhibition itself.

Drawings for sculptures like 'Constructed Head 2' are representational in that they project an imagined work that was to be constructed. The technique is appropriate because that work would itself be representational, although partially abstracted. But in the process of construction the work moved quite a long way from the sketches.

Drawings in the next phase of kinetic – monumental sculptures also seem to be preparatory visualisations of structures but some do not represent the work to be made in the same way. Some are freely drawn in a cubistic way and are quite close to contemporary drawings by the architect Ladovski and the painter Rodchenko. Others are more disciplined and have the air of mechanical drawings, executed with set-square and compass. But their originality can be shown by comparing them with the more literal minded studies for constructions by Gustav Klucis who was informally a pupil of Gabo. Gabo's contain lines, angles and curves that are incomplete in the sense that they do not enclose planes or silhouettes and therefore cannot be constructed literally. They seem, rather, to indicate possible positions of elements, directions of movement and rhythmic features. Moreover, a line that may be, in one sense, a representation of a movement in space can also be developed as an independent arabesque in the plane of the paper on which it is drawn.

Many later drawings are arabesques in the sense that a line may be a complex, open ended curve. Gabo often traced and redrew these lines, refining the curves until they had the right expressive dynamic. In this form they could be used directly in two-dimensional works and more indirectly in three-dimensional constructions. Curvatures were treated by Gabo as objects. He might sketch a line, enlarge it and sharpen it by using a set of french curves in order to fair one arc into another. The resulting form might be transferred to plastic sheet and sawn out. It would be smoothed and its curvature refined. This could then act as a profile to be drawn round or act as guide to an engraving tool or it could be incorporated into a model.

In other cases it seems that Gabo began with a small model, 'drawing' direct into plastic, card or metal by cutting it. He might afterwards make accurate 'engineering' drawings for parts and reconstruct a model in a more refined form, trying out materials to be used.

The next stage would be to produce full scale, dimensional drawings or templates which could be used by himself or by a fabricator to form the parts. There are virtually no drawings for the whole assembly which would be done by Gabo himself, or helped by an assistant under his eye. Perspectival drawings of complete constructions seem generally to have been executed after the construction itself, for example, as an *aide-memoire,* as the starting point for a possible variation or to show the work in a setting.

Drawings for works in stone or for two-dimensional works seem more conventional as preparatory sketches, although Graham Williams has shown that he used plastic figures (that could have been parts of constructed sculptures or parts cut for such sculptures) as templates to profile the stone or to guide the engraving tool.

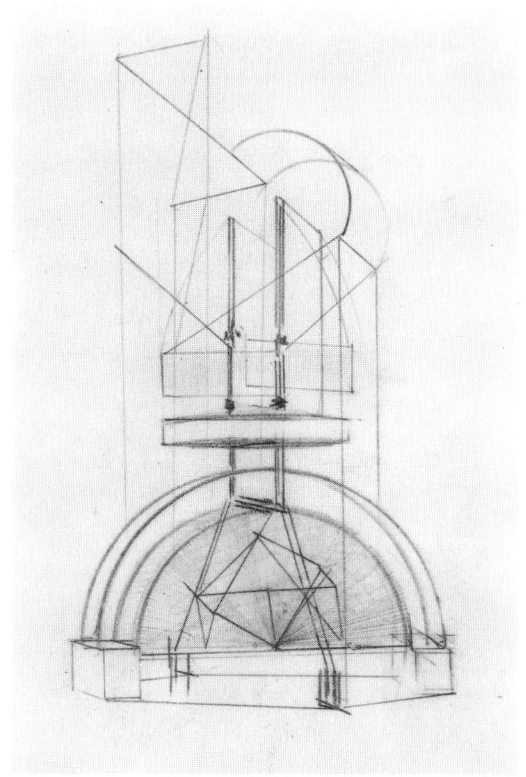

Sketch of a Construction *c.*1922

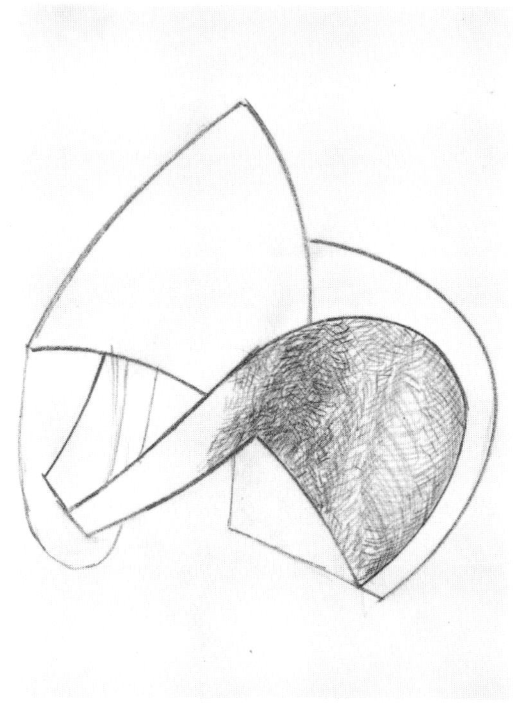

Sketch of Curved Form 1940s? *Famil*

The display includes examples of some of these kinds of drawing including drawing on models and model making as a way of drawing.

The biggest group shows how he explored the basic idea of Spheric Theme, varying the profile of the elements by cutting, extending and redrawing them, how he added to the elements, and altered the fixing points and torsions, but we have not found a complete set for any work. The exhibition itself contains, in addition, six sculptures developed from the idea and several more drawings. It was probably his most fruitful idea.

Architecture and Design

Gabo's biggest architectural project was his entry for the International competition for the Palace of the Soviets, 1929–31. The competition was for a huge conference building on the site of a cathedral, by the river near the Kremlin. It was to be a manifestation of international Communism, and a counter to the League of Nations building to be erected in Switzerland – also the subject of a competition. There was an immense number of entrants including many of the most ambitious architects through-out the world. The eventual winning project was for a vast tower in the form of a base to a giant figure of Lenin. Gabo's contribution was not awarded a prize but was a carefully worked out and elegant design that could have produced a beautiful building.

Its plan comprised two, roughly elliptical, auditoria divided by a tower. It may have been a development of the design by the Vesnin brothers for a Palace of Work, 1922–23. But its elevation is strikingly different. The two auditoria are not embedded in tall cylindrical masses but emerge as partially cantilevered forms like clam-shells. The drawings for it are some of the most beautiful that Gabo ever produced.

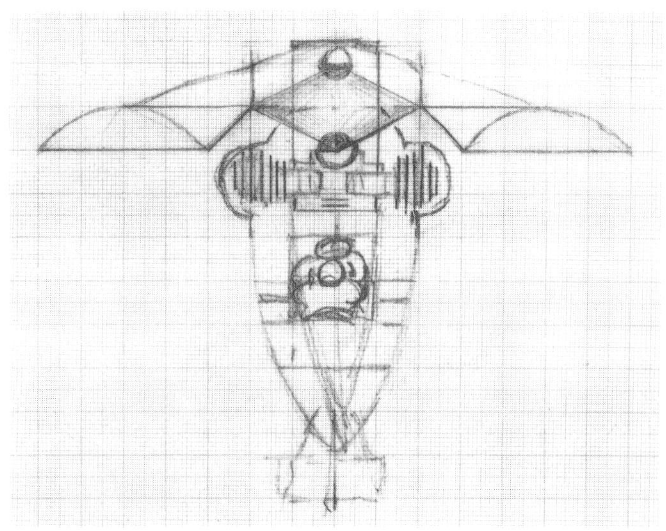

Sketch of vertical take-off aeroplane 1920s
Family Collection

In addition, he devised for it a triangulated roof structure capable of covering such great areas without columns. In the same period he drew an apartment block for the Novembergruppe exhibition in Berlin and town plans. He imagined vast tower blocks, supporting airfields, a re-current dream of the early twentieth century. He even began to draw vertical take-off aeroplanes and helicopters. When he came to England in 1937 he turned to less ambitious projects, designing details for the s.s. Queen Mary (not shown) and a car-body, 1943–44, for the Jowett company. This design was worked out fully in collaboration with the company draftsmen and stylists but never constructed. With its rounded forms it looks forward to post-war car design.

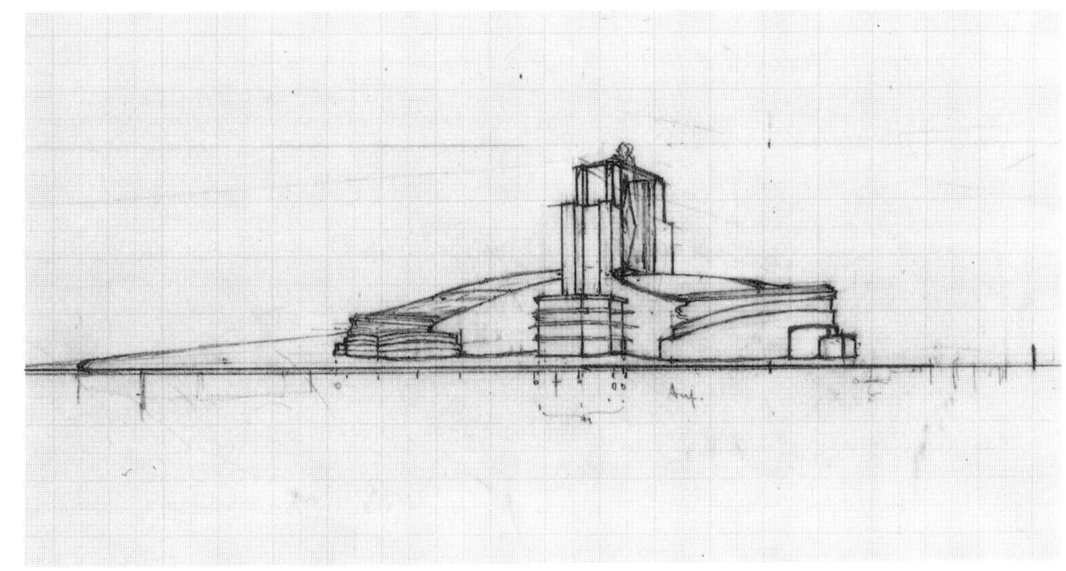

**Sketch of Palace of
the Soviets** *c.*1929
Family Collection

Gabo: Mathematics & Science

Gabo has been considered an intellectual .but he was essentially an imaginative artist and a practical one, creating as he worked with eyes and hands. His writings are eloquent and passionate; they show an acutely perceptive intelligence rather than one which theorises in order to produce work. He did, however, think hard about that work, and he was always aware of what he was doing. Moreover his concept of an artist as one who forms and articulates the consciousness of his time and of the future was linked to his understanding of the great scientific movements of his day and underpinned by a degree of technical assurance acquired as a student of technology in Munich between 1910 and 1913.

The subject of this note is the function of science and mathematics in Gabo's art which has two interrelated aspects – their role as a theme or inspiration and their role as a means. In addition one may point to certain analogies between Gabo's artistic procedures and those in the technical culture of the twentieth century.

From the first we can see that Gabo did not use scientific concepts or technical devices literally. He described his first series of heads and torsos of 1915–17 as 'stereometric'. Stereometry is a branch of mathematics concerned with the description of three-dimensional objects and calculations related to these. One may typically divide an object into notional parallel slices in order to calculate a volume but in the stereometric cube (fig.1) which Gabo made to explain the principle on which these works were made, the divisions cross one another in the diagonal. Although all the angles of the cube are represented, the volume and other properties would have been rather more difficult to calculate. On the other hand the internal space of the cube is laid open and this was what Gabo wanted.

Gabo had probably seen mathematical models in which a volume is constructed from algebraic equations – the converse of practical stereometry. A set had been published by a German mathematician, Brill (fig.2). These were in card so that they could be folded up (like some of Gabo's models). If he had seen one like that later published in *Cahiers d'Art*, 1936, by Man Ray (fig.3), he would have been interested, for this shows planes at right angles to the curved surface, and radiating from an inner axis. That is more or less how Gabo made his early figures, but, in Brill's conventional mathematical models, the planes merely represent rectilinear coordinates like those of a simple graph.

This distinction leads to a practical point. According to his brother Alexei, Gabo was to enlarge the parts of his models using a 'plamimeter' (in translation). This may have been what we call a pantograph, which is a mechanical

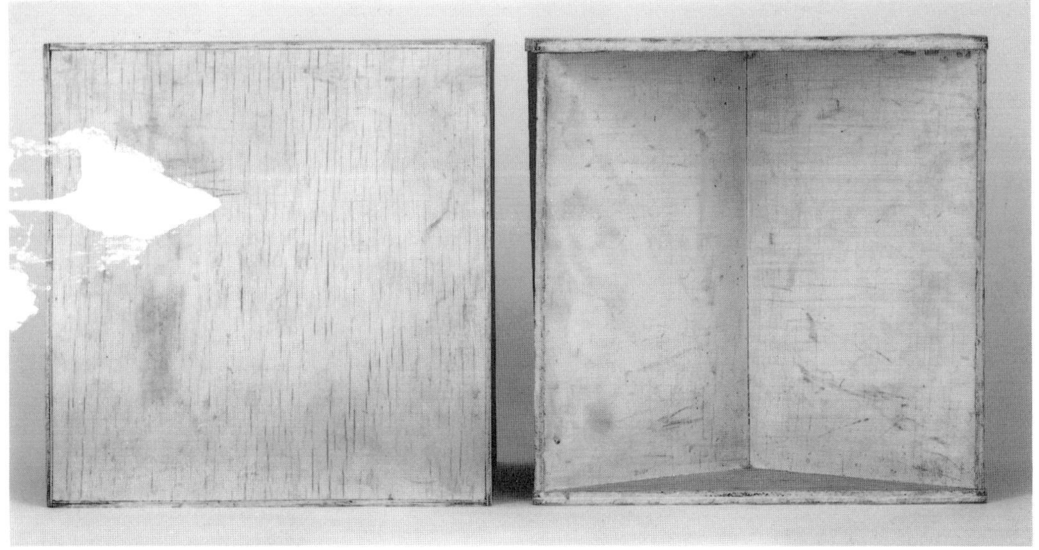

fig.1 Two Cubes demonstrating the 'Stereometric' method 1930

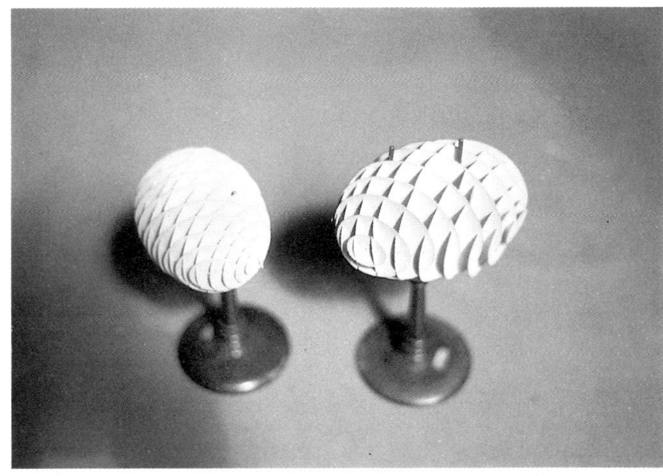

fig.2 Mathematical models in card published by A.Brill, Darmstadt 1874.

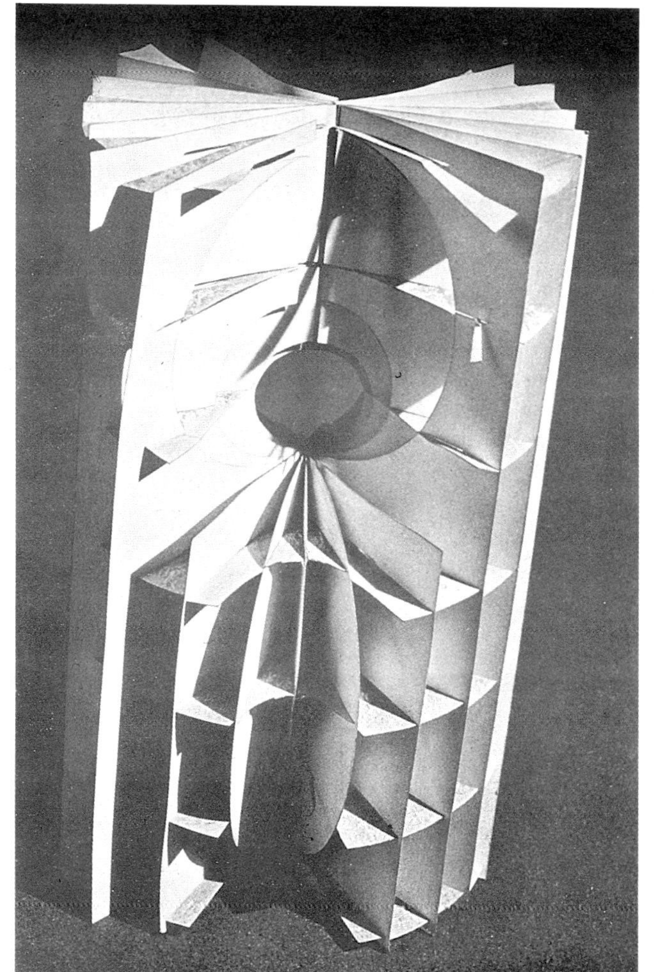

fig.3 Mathematical model in the Institut Poincaré, Paris, from *Cahiers d'Art*, 1936

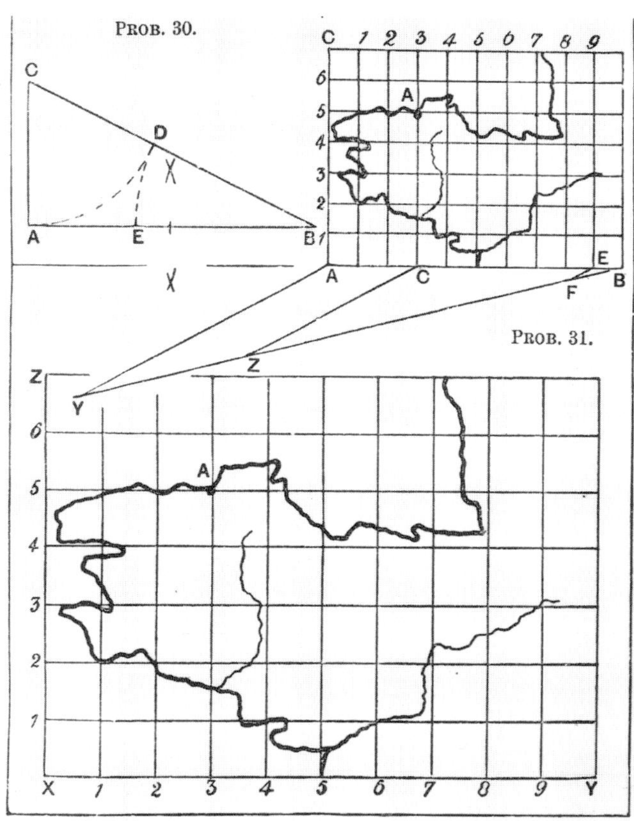

fig.4 Figure from I.H.Morris *Geometrical Drawing for Art Students* 1908 showing methods of enlarging by squaring up.

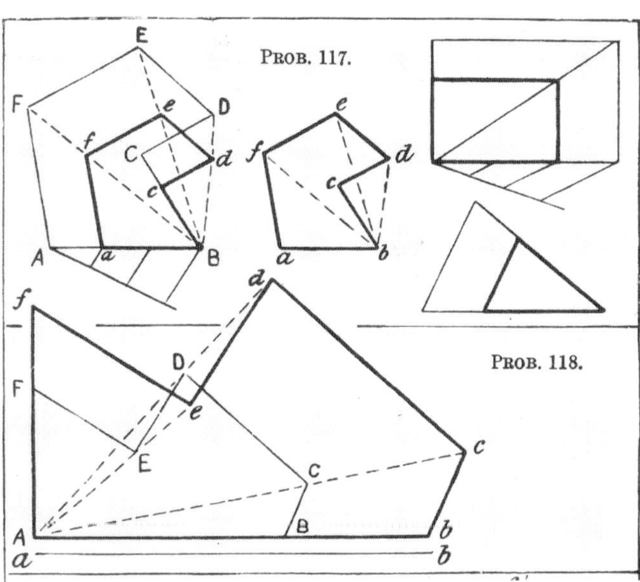

fig.5 Figure from I.H.Morris *Geometrical Drawing for Art Students* 1908 showing method of enlarging by proportionate projection along dotted lines.

device for doing what he later did by hand – extending a form proportionately from a point. It was a method taught to design and art students (fig.5) but rarely used by artists who favoured that of 'squaring up' (fig.4) which is more appropriate for complex forms on a flat plane. But for Gabo's wedge-shaped planes it was both the most convenient and, as a technique, it was the most expressive of the idea of form growing from inside, which is so characteristic of these early works.

There is also a hint of engineering in the form of these sculptures: the predominantly triangulated structure of webs, one that would produce a light and rigid form. But the essence of the metaphor that the method of construction affords is the insight that masses are full of space. On the one hand scientists had shown that solid objects were largely voids between minute particles and, on the other, the terms used by mathematicians to describe the forms of masses were identical to those used to describe voids – in these terms space is as concrete as an object (an intuition of cubist art).

During the post revolutionary fervour Gabo was for a while caught up in the general enthusiasm for technics. But in terms of his use of mathematical concepts he regressed in the twenties, to the traditional norm represented by the simple figures of the most familiar Euclidean geometry. This may have been because he wanted to stress the universality of form against the fashionable progressive symbolism of the machine. At the same time, however, he took to new industrial materials, including plastics, and from this time was never shy of revealing the screws, brackets and other devices that supported his works. They are usually clearly distinct from the elements that comprise the essential form of the work but are constructed with equal care. There is a parallel with the supporting elements of some mathematical models (fig.7), but the analogy is certainly extrinsic.

In the thirties we may discern a renewed interest in a scientific notion as a theme in his work. This was the idea of curved space. Gabo did not know or did not use the classical representations of this but in general terms it did appeal to him and seems to have partly prompted the invention of forms which first appear, strangely enough, in stone carving. The forms not only curve but seem to swallow one another – one space penetrates another. In 1937 he went so far as to make a free variation on an actual mathematical model of a complex space (illustrated in the catalogue, p.35) and continued by using strings to define curved surfaces in a manner derived from other such models (fig.7). But these afforded him merely a new material – the use to which he put it was, as always, expressive rather than literal.

He showed, as other artists have, a passing interest in the Moebius band – a classical figure in the relatively new mathematics of topology – but he seems to have realised that it would not serve directly and preferred the topologically more unsophisticated two-sided plane of, say, the

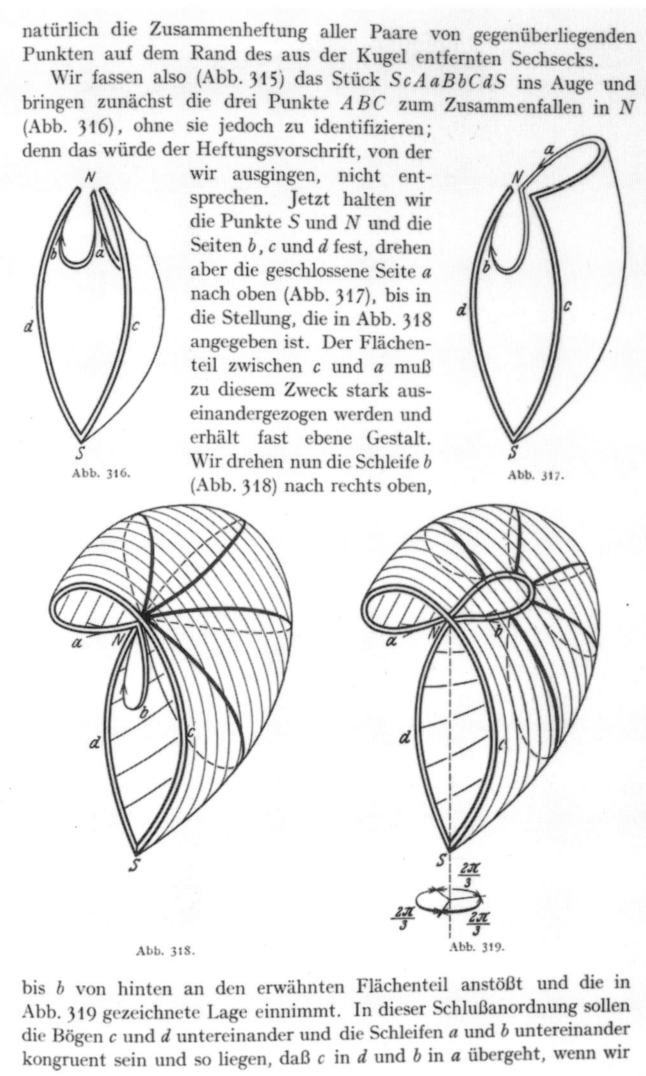

natürlich die Zusammenheftung aller Paare von gegenüberliegenden Punkten auf dem Rand des aus der Kugel entfernten Sechsecks.

Wir fassen also (Abb. 315) das Stück $ScAaBbCdS$ ins Auge und bringen zunächst die drei Punkte ABC zum Zusammenfallen in N (Abb. 316), ohne sie jedoch zu identifizieren; denn das würde der Heftungsvorschrift, von der wir ausgingen, nicht entsprechen. Jetzt halten wir die Punkte S und N und die Seiten b, c und d fest, drehen aber die geschlossene Seite a nach oben (Abb. 317), bis in die Stellung, die in Abb. 318 angegeben ist. Der Flächenteil zwischen c und a muß zu diesem Zweck stark auseinandergezogen werden und erhält fast ebene Gestalt. Wir drehen nun die Schleife b (Abb. 318) nach rechts oben,

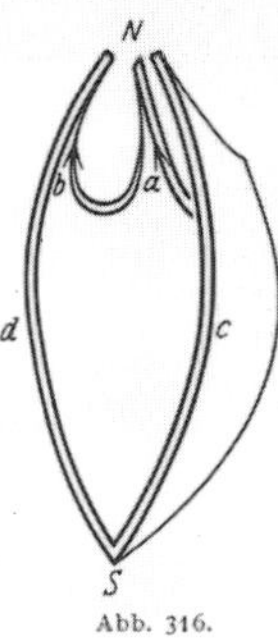

Abb. 316.

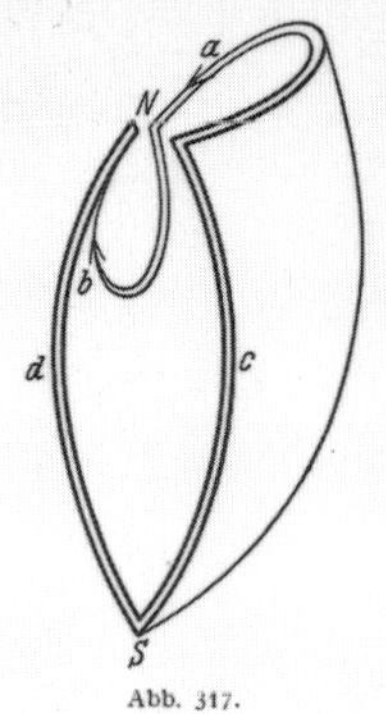

Abb. 317.

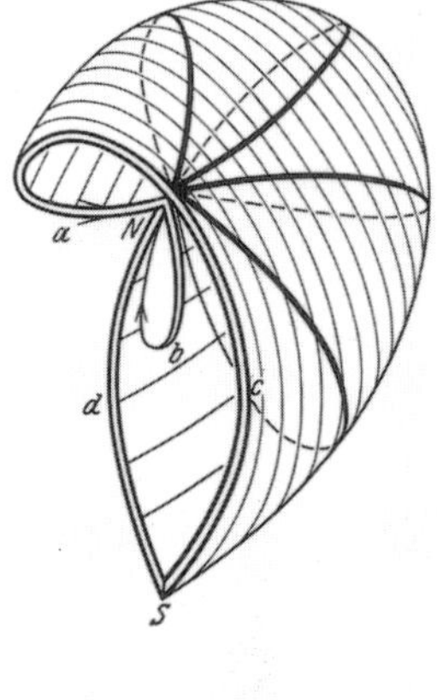

Abb. 318.

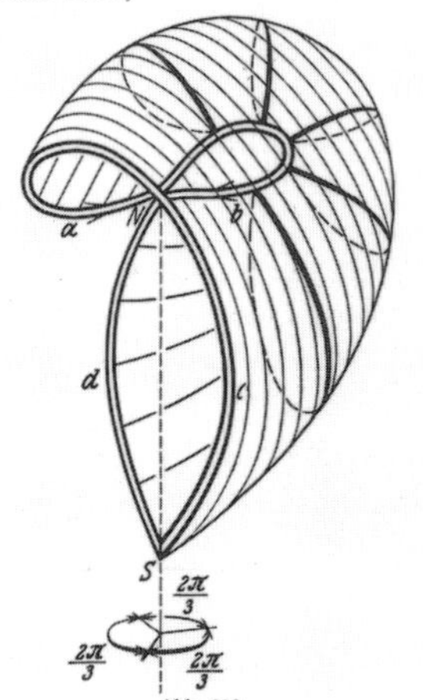

Abb. 319.

bis b von hinten an den erwähnten Flächenteil anstößt und die in Abb. 319 gezeichnete Lage einnimmt. In dieser Schlußanordnung sollen die Bögen c und d untereinander und die Schleifen a und b untereinander kongruent sein und so liegen, daß c in d und b in a übergeht, wenn wir

fig.6 D.Hilbert and S.Cohn-Vassen topological diagram from *Die Grundlehren der mathematische Wissenischaften* 1932 showing 'Boy Planes' of complex curvature. Although almost certainly unknown to Gabo these show a certain convergence of mathematical forms with those of art in the period.

spherical themes. However the strung surfaces of some sculptures seem to provide an alternative, twisted 'Moebius' space.

In sculpture, curved space, in Einstein's sense, is not to be distinguished from curvature *in* space, and Gabo characteristically concentrated on what was expressible – above all rhythm in form and space. The analogy between the forms of his sculpture and the diagramatic representation of molecules, galaxies, shells or cell formations was no more and no less than a metaphor of universal will to form – he had no need and no desire to imitate such forms, for the essence of his art was that it was constructed on its own terms.

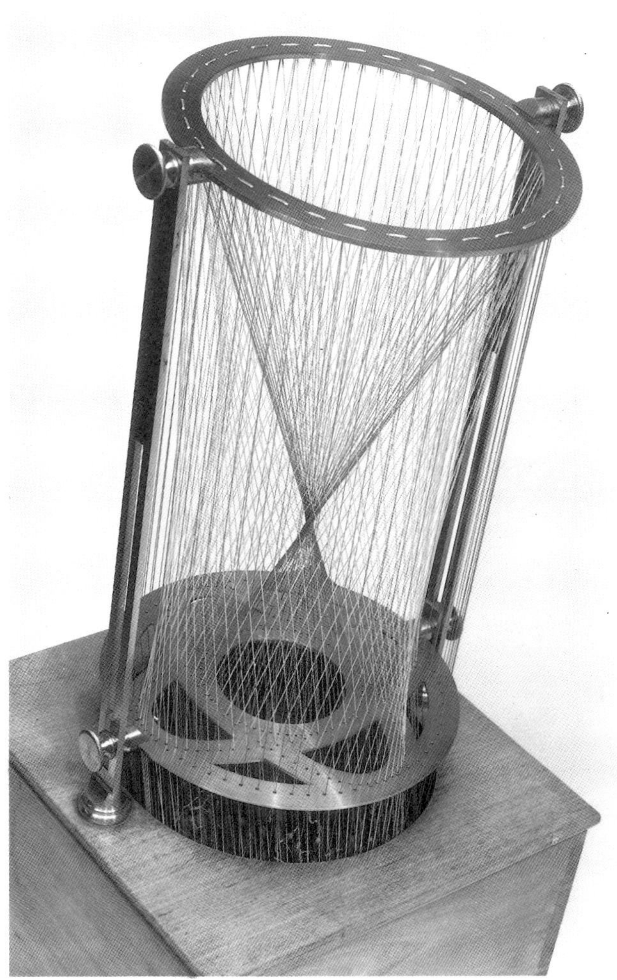

fig.7 Stringed mathematical model in Science Museum,
London, Lagrange 1872.

There is no sign in Gabo's writings that he considered
the concept of symmetry to be a peculiarly potent one in
the science of his time and equally no hint that its importance in his own art had anything to do with its mathematical expression. Indeed, looking at his drawings,
models and partly worked materials, we can see that his
use of symmetry was, like everything else, imaginative,
practical and based in art. But his constructive method
gave him the ambition and scope to manipulate forms and
objects freely and so he arrived at an extended notion of
symmetry. He made use of symmetries: positive-negative,
right-left handed, or up-down, and often form-matrix, as
well as single and multiple axes.

What made him a man of his century, specifically in this
respect, and set him apart from many other artists, was
that he could generate new 'truths' by playing with such
terms.

Models and Constructions

From the beginning Gabo made models for his sculpture that were capable of being constructed on almost any scale and in any suitable material, usually sheet metal or plastic.

Although, of course, models or maquettes have been a familiar element of the practice of art from the fifteenth century at least, they are, relatively, a rarity in the modern period. In the field of painting, sketches have almost disappeared, especially in abstract art, since the work is created most often by a direct process in which the medium and the momentary states of the work in progress prompt new responses in the painter until the picture seems complete. Carved, modelled and welded sculpture offers the same mutuality to the artist, even when working on quite a large scale. But Gabo had resolved to be a constructor, often of very complex works, and, paradoxically, it was the making of a model that allowed him, too, to work in this way. He could cut, try out, adjust and glue up his model until it took the form that satisfied his imagination. Then he could take it all to pieces, scale it up, cut fresh materials to shape and assemble a pristine and apparently effortless work.

The making of models was a means, in most cases, of clarifying an idea so that it could be created accurately on any appropriate scale, and so that it could be stored for use directly or with variations. From the parts of the model, templates or elements of the sculpture could be exactly specified so that the artist himself or a fabricator could form the parts of the work. This might imply that the work was considered as a set of point relations in space – its meaning resided essentially in these relationships – curvatures, symmetries, transformations. Such a set of relationships is expressive in itself of Gabo's intuition of the work and of the thought which creates our world. But the relationships were not a logical or mathematical formulation; they were worked out and manifested in the material world and the material form which they could variously take, its properties and associations were equally a part of the work.

The notion of construction itself implies the possibility of architectural scale and was inextricably linked with Gabo's optimistic and heroic view of the role of the artist as formulator of the world of the future. But from the thirties, when the industrial Utopianism of the early century had lost its charm and when Gabo's sensibility had become gentler and subtler, his sense of scale also seems to become more specific. The work was to be not only a flawless and perfectly expressive form but a form related to its setting.

This may have been partly because he had a real chance to work practically on a large scale. His models were still expanded to human or monumental proportion but their detail and texture were adjusted to their context. Certain works assert themselves more clearly as specific pieces of sculpture than those of the twenties and are distinguished by their organic forms from most contemporary architecture. Monumental works, especially up to about 1940, had often been imagined as fountains or placed in parks; the man-made forms would be complementary to those determined by natural forces. Later works, themselves more obviously organic, were devised to complement the man-made architectural spaces. Very large works like the Bijenkorf sculpture are animated by internal detail and texture.

The progression in scale is not always from small model to large sculpture. Gabo's practice of reworking and developing tried themes led him to make models after the fact so that he could treat them, almost as a sculptor does his stone, cutting and reshaping. But he was an artist who thought much with his hands, constantly working back and forth between concept and realisation. Making models was his way of developing a thought from one work to the next.

The interrelated choice of a scale and of the materials to be used was in Gabo's work as expressive as the performance of a play or musical composition.

List of Works

Dimensions are given where known. Unless otherwise stated, they are given in centimetres: height × width × depth. For some works the relevance of width and depth measurements is questionable. For these only a single dimension is given such as height, or the height plus one other dimension such as diameter.

Sculptures

1 **Constructed Head No.1**
1915/reassembled 1985
Plywood, 53.3 high
Family collection

2 **Constructed Head No.2** 1916
Galvanised iron, 45 high
Family Collection

3 **Constructed Head No.2** 1916/1923–4
Ivory rhodoid, 43 high
*Dallas Museum of Art, gift of
The Edward S. Marcus Memorial Fund*

4 **Constructed Head No.2** 1916/1966
Cor-ten steel painted grey, 178 high
Family Collection

5 **Constructed Head No.3 (Head in a
Corner Niche)** 1917/1964
Phosphor-bronze, 62.2 × 70 × 35
Family Collection

6 **Model for 'Constructed Torso'**
1917/reassembled 1981
Cardboard, 39.5 high
Family Collection

7 **Maquette for 'Constructed Torso'**
1917–8/reassembled 1985
Cardboard, 117 high
Family Collection

8 **Kinetic Construction (Standing Wave)**
1919–20/reconstructed 1985
Metal rod with electric motor, 61.5 high
Tate Gallery

9 **Model for 'Column'** 1920–1
Celluloid and other plastic, 14.4 high
Tate Gallery

10 **Column** 1922–3/c.1947
Perspex on aluminium base, 28.2 high
Family Collection

11 **Column** 1922–3/1975
Glass, perspex and stainless steel,
193 high
Family Collection

12 **Square Relief** 1920–1/1937
Perspex on aluminium base,
44.5 × 44.5 × 16.5
Family Collection

13 **Model for a Fountain**
1923–4/reassembled 1985
Glass (replaced) and enamelled metal
(repainted), 72.5 high
*Art Gallery of Ontario, gift of the Gabo
Family in honour of the Volunteer
Committee's 40th Anniversary, 1986*

14 **Construction in Space: Diagonal**
1921–5/reassembled 1986
Glass, metal celluloid, 62.2 high
Family Collection

15 **Construction in Space; Vertical**
1923–5/reassembled 1986
Glass, painted brass (and plastic), 120 high
Family Collection

16 **Model for 'Construction in Space with
Balance on Two Points**
c.1924–5/reassembled 1978–9
Celluloid on plastic base, 13.5 × 18.2
Family Collection

17 **Construction in Space with Balance on
Two Points** 1924–5/reassembled 1982
Plexiglass, 27 × 37
Family Collection

18 **Model for 'Rotating Fountain'** 1925/
reassembled 1986
Metal, celluloid (and other plastics),
54 high
Family Collection

19 **Monument for an Airport**
1924–6 reassembled 1985
Glass (replaced) enamelled brass,
aluminium (repainted) and wood,
49.5 × 73.3 × c.30
Family Collection

20 **Circular Relief** 1925–8
Plastic on wooden base,
23 deep × 50 diameter
Tate Gallery

21 **Red Cavern** c.1926
Celluloid and/or rhodoid, glass, metal,
and cork in wooden box, 66 high
Tate Gallery

22 **Model for Stage Set for 'La Chatte'**
1926–7/reassembled and restored 1987
Metal, plastics, wood and cloth,
61 × 54.5 × 79.5
Tate Gallery

23 **Model for 'Construction in Space:
Two Cones'** 1927/altered 1932–7
Celluloid, 8.3 × 12.4
Tate Gallery

24 **Construction in Space: 'Two Cones'**
1968
Plastic on white marble base, 26.7 high
Tate Gallery

25 **Model for 'Torsion'** 1928–9
Plastic, 8.9 × 9.5 diameter
Tate Gallery

26 **Model for 'Double Relief in a Niche'**
1929–30
Plastic, cork and cardboard,
11.4 × 22.2 × 5.1
Tate Gallery

27 **Construction in a Niche** 1930
Plastic, metals and cork in wooden box,
61 high
Tate Gallery

28 **Construction in Space: Soaring**
1929–30/reassembled 1985
Brass painted black and white plexiglass
cones (replaced), 90 high
Family Collection

29 **Construction in Space: Arch** 1929/1937
Rhodoid with plexiglass substitutions on
perspex base, 46.4 × 76.2 × 21.6
Family Collection

30 **Monument for an Airport** c.1932/1948
Perspex with brass painted black,
41.6 × 108 × 57.5
Family Collection

31 **Construction: Stone with a Collar** 1933
Stone, ivory, rhodoid, brass strip painted
black, 40 × 72
Family Collection

32 **Kinetic Stone Carving** 1936–44
Portland stone, 24 × 37
Family Collection

33 **Model for 'Spheric Theme'** 1936–7
Perspex, 10.2 diameter
Family Collection

34 **Model for 'Spheric Construction:
Fountain'** 1937–8
Perspex, 9.5 high
Family Collection

35 **Spheric Theme: Black Variation** 1937
Rhodoid and black celluloid, 42.5 diameter
Family Collection

36 **Spheric Theme: 2nd Variation** 1937–8
Perspex, 43.5 high
Family Collection

37 **Spheric Theme: Transparent Variation**
c.1937
Celluloid and perspex, 21.5 diameter
Family Collection

38 **Spheric Theme (Penetrated Variation)**
1963–5
Bronze, 33 high
Tate Gallery

39 **Bronze Spheric Theme** 1960/1965
Bronze with bronze springwire, 92 high
Tate Gallery

40 **Construction on a Plane** 1927
Perspex and celluloid on perspex and
wood base, 48 × 48 × 19.6
Family Collection

41 **Construction on a Line** 1937
Perspex and celluloid, 43.4 × 43.6 × 19.2
Family Collection

42 **Model for 'Construction in Space:
Crystal'** 1937
Celluloid, 7.6 × 7.6 × 3.8
Tate Gallery

43 **Construction in Space: Crystal** 1937–9
Rhodoid, 22 × 27 × 18
Family Collection

44 **Construction in Space with Crystalline
Centre** 1938–40
Perspex and celluloid, 32.4 × 47
Family Collection

45 **Marble Carving** 1938/1966–67
Portuguese marble mounted in Perspex
on stainless steel base, 107 × 76.4 × 10.4
Family Collection

46 **Construction in Space with Rose Marble Carving (Variation No.2)** 1938/9
Rose marble, mounted in perspex, 81 × 81
Family Collection

47 **Spiral Theme** 1941
Plastic, 14 high
Tate Gallery

48 **Linear Construction in Space No.1**
1942/1945–9
Perspex with nylon filament,
61.3 × 61.3 × 13
*Art Gallery of Ontario, gift from the
Volunteer Committee Fund 1986*

49 **Linear Construction in Space No.1**
1942/c.1970
Perspex with nylon filament on perspex
base,
Family Collection

50 **Linear Construction in Space No. 1
(Variation)** 1956/7
Perspex with nylon monofilament,
45.3 × 45.3 × 17.9
Owen and Sonja Franklin

51 **Linear Construction in Space No. 1
(Variation)** 1942–3/1976
Perspex with nylon monofilament,
21.9 × 21.9
Family Collection

52 **Linear Construction in Space No. 2**
1949/1972–3
Perspex with nylon monofilament,
92 high
Family Collection

53 **Linear Construction in Space No. 2**
1949/c.1976
Perspex with nylon monofilament,
38.1 long
Family Collection

54 **Optical Relief** 1951–67
Aluminium, plastic, stainless steel spring-
wire and paint on wood base, 81 × 47 × 51
Family Collection

55 **Construction in Space, with Net**
1951–52
Phosphor bronze wire mesh, aluminium,
perspex, and mixed media, 63.6 high
*Art Gallery of Ontario, purchased with
assistance from the Volunteer Committee
Fund, 1986*

56 **Model for a 'Monument to the
Unknown Political Prisoner'** 1952
Plastic with stainless steel wire mesh on
plastic and slate base, 41 high
Tate Gallery

57 **Model for 'Linear Construction in
Space No.3 with Red'** 1952
Plastic with nylon thread, 9.5 high
Tate Gallery

58 **Repose** 1953
Carrara marble on base of perspex,
aluminium and wood, 15 high
Family Collection

59 **Final Model for the Bijenkorf
Construction, Rotterdam** 1955
Brass, copper and steel on black marble
base, 145 high
Gilbert de Botton, Switzerland

60 **Linear Construction in Space No.4**
1955/c.1970
Phosphor bronze with stainless steel and
phosphor-bronze spring-wire on
phosphor-bronze base, 78.7 high
Family Collection

61 **Linear Construction in Space No.4** 1970
Aluminium with stainless steel spring wire,
68 × 13 × 211.5
*Musée National d'Art Moderne, Centre
Georges Pompidou, Paris*

62 **Construction in Space: Suspended**
1957/1962
Perspex nylon monofilament, red and
black paint, gold-plated stainless steel
cradle on stainless steel base,
30.5 × 28 × 28
Family Collection

63 **Construction in Space: Suspended**
1957/1965
Perspex, nylon filament, gilded phosphor-
bronze cradle, on aluminium base,
51.3 × 61.6 × 52.7
Family Collection

64 **Construction in Space: Suspended
(Variation)** 1957/c.1971
Perspex, nylon monofilament,
phosphor-bronze cradle on aluminium and
perspex base, 53 × 61.9 × 55.9
Family Collection

65 **Construction in Space: Arch No.2**
1958/1963
Phosphor-bronze, copper and stainless
steel spring-wire, on wood base, 82.6 high
Family Collection

66 **Torsion, Variation** 1962/1963
Phosphor-bronze with stainless steel
spring-wire, wood base, 73.1 high
Family Collection

67 **Torsion, Variation** 1962/c.1974–5
Stainless steel with stainless steel
spring-wire, 136.5 high
Family Collection

68 **Vertical Construction No.1** 1962/1967
Phosphor-bronze with stainless steel and
black spring-wire on wood, 203 high
Family Collection

69 **White Stone** 1963–4
Grey marble, 46 high
Family Collection

70 **Quartz Stone** 1964–5
Portuguese marble, 80 high
Family Collection

71 **Granite Carving** 1964–5
Granite, 63.5 × 61
Family Collection

72 **Red Stone** 1964–5
African red stone, 24 × 45
Family Collection

73 **Torsion (Project for a Fountain)** 1965
Bronze, 76.2 high
Tate Gallery

74 **Bronze Spheric Theme (Variation)**
1964–6
Phosphor-bronze with stainless steel
spring-wire on bronze base, 99 × 68
Family Collection

75 **Model for 'Bronze Spheric Theme'**
c.1966–7
Phosphor-bronze with stainless steel and
spring-wire, 20.5 high
Family Collection

76 **Spheric Theme** 1967/1969–71
Stainless steel, 24 high
*Staatliche Museen Preussischer
Kulturbesitz, Nationalgalerie, Berlin*

77 **Vertical Construction No.2**
1964–5/1969–70
Stainless steel with stainless steel
spring-wire, set into motorized base,
292 high
Family Collection

78 **Monument to the Astronauts**
started c.1966
Brass, plastic and stainless steel gauze,
54.3 × 54.7
Family Collection

Drawings, Paintings and Prints

79 **Christmas** c.1910–12
Pastel, 36.3 × 45
Family Collection

80 **Hamlet** 1912
Watercolour and pencil, 14.2 × 11
Family Collection

81 **Young Girl** 1912
Watercolour and pencil, 17.9 × 13.9
Family Collection

82 **Girl in a Low Necked Dress** 1912
Watercolour and pencil, 16.6 × 18.3
Family Collection

83 **Kneeling Figure** c.1915
Pencil and charcoal, 51 × 36
Family Collection

84 **Study for 'Head No.1'** 1915
Pencil, 19 × 17
Family Collection

85 **Studies for 'Head No.2'** 1915
Pencil, 39.5 × 50.2
Family Collection

86 **Study for 'Head No.2'** 1915
Blue pencil, 18 × 11
Family Collection

87 **Studies for 'Head No.2'** 1915
Pencil, 43.5 × 34.5
Family Collection

88 **Study for a Constructed Head** 1916
Pencil, 19 × 17
Family Collection

89 **Sketch of a Nude** c.1915–16
Pencil, 29 × 30
Family Collection

90 **Sketch of a Figure** c.1915–16
Ink, 21.8 × 14.1
Family Collection

91 **Nude Study** c.1915–16
Ink, 12.6 × 14.2
Family Collection

92 **Studies of Kneeling Figure** 1916
Pencil, 39.5 × 50
Family Collection

93 **Study for 'Torso'** 1916
Pencil,
Family Collection

94 **Study for 'Head in a Corner Niche'**
*c.*1916–17
Ink, 14 × 12.5
Family Collection

95 **Studies of Mother and Child** *c.*1916–17
Pencil, 30 × 26.5
Family Collection

96 **Tower Project** 1917
Charcoal and pencil, 41.2 × 31.5
Family Collection

97 **Study for an Outdoor Constructon**
1917
Pencil, 23 × 23.5
Family Collection

98 **Study for a Tower** *c.*1917
Pencil, 40.3 × 28.5
Family Collection

99 **Study of a Head** *c.*1917–18
Pencil and pastel, 35.8 × 22.2
Dallas Museum of Art

100 **Study for a Relief** *c.*1917–19
Pencil, 48 × 35
Family Collection

101 **Study for a Relief Construction**
*c.*1917–19
Pencil, 17.9 × 14.5
Tate Gallery

102 **Study for a Construction on a Stairway**
1918
Pencil, 44 × 32
Family Collection

103 **Design for a Construction** 1918
Pencil, 40.5 × 27.3
Family Collection

104 **Sketch** *c.*1918–19
Pencil and crayon, 24.3 × 20.4
Tate Gallery

105 **Sketch for a Square in Moscow** 1919
Pencil, 45 × 35
Thomas P. Whitney Collection

106 **Design for a Kinetic Construction**
*c.*1922
Pencil and ink, 25 × 21
Family Collection

107 **Study for a Relief** after 1922
Pencil, 25 × 21
Family Collection

108 **Study for a Tower Construction** 1923
Pencil, 34 × 22.2
Family Collection

109 **Study for 'Model for a Fountain'** *c.*1923
Pencil, 21.5 × 16
*Art Gallery of Ontario, gift from Graham
and Nina Williams in recognition of
Dr Alan Wilkinson*

110 **Study for a Tower Fountain** 1924
Pencil, 20.5 × 21
Family Collection

111 **Architectural Project** 1924
Pencil and charcoal, 65 × 50
Family Collection

112 **Architectural Project** 1925
Watercolour, ink and pencil, 22.6 × 40.2
Family Collection

113 **Studies for Architecture and 'Spheric
Theme'** 1925–26
Pencil, 54.7 × 50
Family Collection

114 **Study for Stage Set 'La Chatte'** 1926
Charcoal, 34.3 × 28
Family Collection

115 **Study for Stage Set 'La Chatte'** 1926
Pencil, 22 × 28
Family Collection

116 **Costume Sketch for 'La Chatte'** 1926
Pencil, 28.3 × 22
Family Collection

117 **Costume Sketch for 'La Chatte'** 1926
Pencil and pastel, 26.7 × 21
Family Collection

118 **Costume Sketch for 'La Chatte'** 1926
Pencil and pastel, 27.3 × 21.5
Family Collection

119 **Costume Sketch for 'La Chatte'** 1926
Pencil and pastel, 25.5 × 19
Family Collection

120 **Sketch, Monte Carlo** 1926
Pencil and crayon, 26.7 × 20.3
Family Collection

121 **Study for a Construction** 1928
Pencil, 28.7 × 25.5
Family Collection

122 **Study for 'Arch No.1'** 1929
Pencil, 21 × 30
Family Collection

123 **Sketch for a Carving in Stone** 1930
Crayon and gouache, 27.3 × 33.7
Family Collection

124 **Front Elevation of the Palace of the
Soviets** 1931
Pencil, 23.2 × 26
Family Collection

125 **Sketch for a Stone Carving** 1933
Pencil and crayon, 16.5 × 15.2
Family Collection

126 **Study for 'Logan Rock (the Urn)'** 1933
Pencil, 29 × 22.5
Family Collection

127 **Untitled** 1930s (?)
Crayon, 39.5 × 25.5
Family Collection

128 **Sketch for a Stone Carving** 1933
Pencil, 14 × 22
Tate Gallery

129 **Sketch for 'Construction through a
Plane'** 1935
Pencil, 24.1 × 20.5
Tate Gallery

130 **Sketch for 'Spheric Theme'** *c.*1935–37
Blue pencil, 19.7 × 32.2
Tate Gallery

131 **Sketch for 'Spheric Theme'** *c.*1937
Pencil and ink, 24 × 20.4
Tate Gallery

132 **Study for 'Construction on a Line'**
*c.*1937
Pencil, 24 × 20.5
Family Collection

133 **Study for 'Construction in Space:
Crystal'** *c.*1937
Pencil, 24 × 20.5
Family Collection

134 **Sketch** 1940
Crayon, 31 × 29
Family Collection

135 **Study with Red** 1941
Mixed media, 27 × 34
Family Collection

136 **Study for an Arch Monument**
Pencil and felt pen, 48.5 × 39.5
Family Collection

137 **Sketch for a Vertical Composition**
*c.*1952
Pencil, 38 × 27
Family Collection

138 **Sketch of the 'Monument to the
Unknown Political Prisoner'** 1954
Pencil, 23.7 × 18.7
Family Collection

139 **Study for a Fountain** 1950s (?)
Pencil and crayon, 34.3 × 42.4
Family Collection

140 **Project for a Colour Lithograph**
(date unknown)
Pastel, 58.5 × 47
Family Collection

141 **Self Portrait** *c.*1907–10
Oil on canvas, 24 × 17
Family Collection

142 **Logan Rock (The Urn)** 1938
Oil on board, 21.5 × 27
Family Collection

143 **Hovering** 1940
Oil on board, 76 × 63.5
Family Collection

144 **The Pilot's View** 1942
Oil on paper, 37 × 27.5
Family Collection

145 **Kinetic Oil Painting in Four
Movements** 1943
Oil on board, 26.5 × 19
Family Collection

146 **Spinning** 1944
Oil on paper, 19.5 × 15.5
Family Collection

147 **Strontium** 1945
Oil on cardboard, 22.5 × 29.5
Family Collection

148 **Turquoise** 1945
Oil on board mounted on motorised
revolving disc, 20.2 × 23.2
Family Collection

149 **Portfolio of twelve wood engravings**
1950–mid 1970s
Monoprinted wood engravings, various
Family Collection

Exhibition Plan

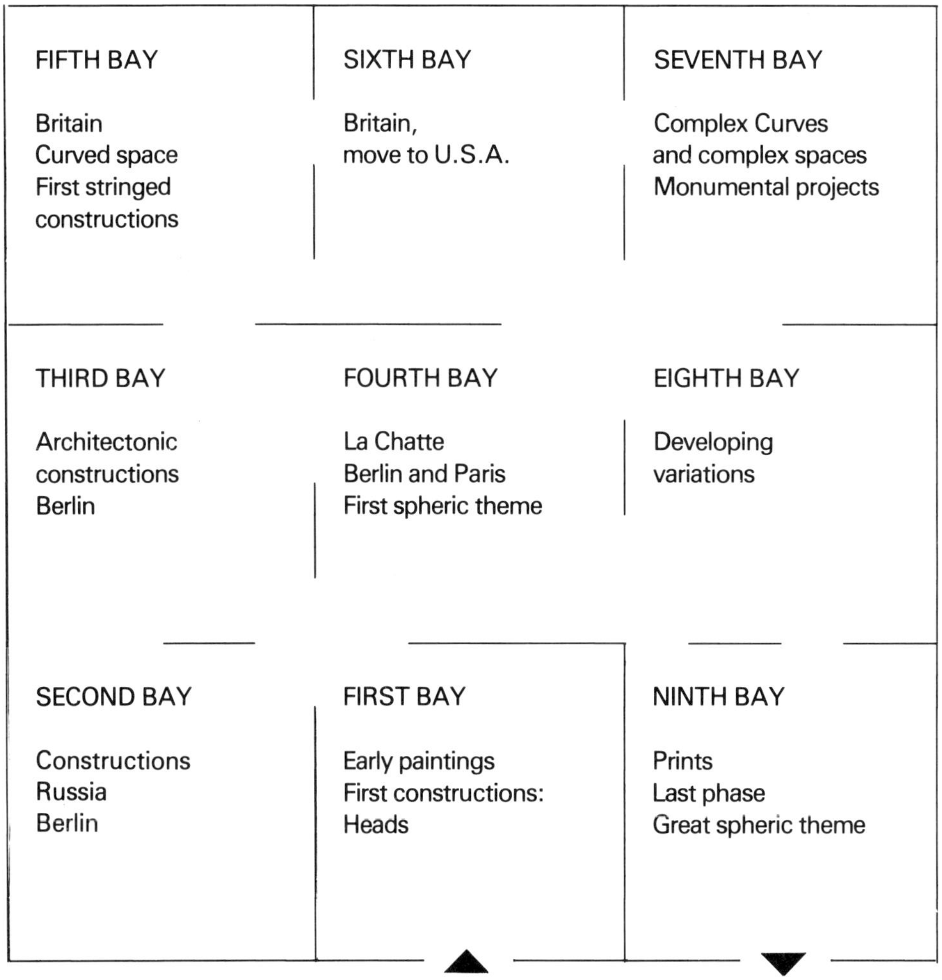

FIFTH BAY	SIXTH BAY	SEVENTH BAY
Britain Curved space First stringed constructions	Britain, move to U.S.A.	Complex Curves and complex spaces Monumental projects
THIRD BAY	FOURTH BAY	EIGHTH BAY
Architectonic constructions Berlin	La Chatte Berlin and Paris First spheric theme	Developing variations
SECOND BAY	FIRST BAY	NINTH BAY
Constructions Russia Berlin	Early paintings First constructions: Heads	Prints Last phase Great spheric theme